Profile
of
Robert Lowell

CHARLES E. MERRILL PROFILES

Under the General Editorship of
Matthew J. Bruccoli and Joseph Katz

Profile
of
Robert Lowell

Compiled by

Jerome Mazzaro

State University of New York at Buffalo

Charles E. Merrill Publishing Company
A Bell & Howell Company
Columbus, Ohio

60535

Printed in the United States of America

Preface

Two recent collections have appeared to make available for readers of Robert Lowell's poetry a quantity of excellent criticism. Both have made possible my assembling in this book a completely different and equally essential collection. If I have neglected the *Paris Review* interview, Randall Jarrell's reviews of *Lord Weary's Castle* and *The Mills of the Kavanaughs*, M. L. Rosenthal's "Robert Lowell and the Poetry of Confession," or Norman Mailer's portrait from *Armies of the Night*, it is that these items are available in either Thomas Parkinson's *Robert Lowell: A Collection of Critical Essays* (1968) or Michael London and Robert Boyers's *Robert Lowell: A Portrait of the Artist in His Time* (1970). Sometimes, as in the cases of Jarrell and Rosenthal, they are in both. I have also shied away from relevant material that is already in book form: Hugh B. Staples's *Robert Lowell: The First Twenty Years* (1962), William Martz's *The Achievement of Robert Lowell* (1966), Jay Martin's *Robert Lowell* (1970), R. K. Meiners's *Everything To Be Endured: An Essay on Robert Lowell and Modern Poetry* (1970), and even my own *The Poetic Themes of Robert Lowell* (1965). My feeling was that these often difficult-to-obtain pieces ought to have priority.

That Lowell should amass in so short a time such a quantity of excellent criticism—and even more may be culled or cited—is a testimonial to his own importance as a poet. Descended from the Reverend Robert Traill Spence Lowell (1816-1891), a minor writer and older brother of James Russell Lowell, he represents a portion of the family excluded from Ferris Greenslet's history of the Lowells, *The Lowells and Their Seven Worlds* (1946), and beyond the scope of Edward Weeks's *The Lowells and Their Institute* (1966). Born on March 1, 1917, he attended first Brimmer School and then St. Mark's, where he had been enrolled since birth and which his great-grandfather had headed from 1869 to 1872. During that time he could not avoid being aware of his cousins—the Winslows or Amy and Lawrence Lowell—or developing an "anti-Bostonianism" which, in *The Problem of Boston* (1966), Martin Green sees as "itself a Bostonian trait." He was lured into becoming a poet at St. Mark's by a reading of Elizabeth Drew's *Discovering Poetry* (1933) and the presence on staff of the poet Richard Eberhart. He spent a brief period at Harvard before going to Kenyon College in 1937 "to study with a man who was a poet," John Crowe Ransom.

In 1940, Lowell took a degree in classics and, in the same year, was converted to Roman Catholicism and married the fiction writer Jean Stafford. Teaching jobs at Kenyon College and Louisiana State University, work as an editorial assistant to Sheed and Ward in New York City, and five months in jail as a conscientious objector followed before his first volume, *Land of Unlikeness,* appeared in 1944 to mixed reviews. His second volume, *Lord Weary's Castle* (1946), was more universally praised. It won him a series of awards including the Pulitzer Prize and established him among critics as a traditionalist and the young American poet to watch. By 1951 and his next volume, *The Mills of the Kavanaughs,* Jean Stafford had divorced him and he had married a second fiction writer, Elizabeth Hardwick. Years of travel, teaching, and personal crises intervened before the birth of a daughter Harriet and, in 1959, his return to publishing with *Life Studies.* This remarkable volume won Lowell a new reputation as a daring experimenter as well as a National Book Award. He went on to earn a share of the Bollingen Prize for Translation two years later with the publication of *Phaedra* and *Imitations.*

For the Union Dead (1964) secured Lowell the place of America's foremost living poet. In the same year he turned to theater with *The Old Glory.* His refusal to attend a White House Arts Festival because of America's involvement in Vietnam became in 1965 a cause célèbre. It marked the beginning of a vigorous political involvement that included participation in the Pentagon March of November 1967, and support for Senator Eugene McCarthy's unsuccessful bid for a presidential nomination in 1968. In 1966, Lowell became the first American poet nominated for the Oxford Chair in Poetry. His last four efforts, *Near the Ocean* (1967), an adaptation of *Prometheus Bound* (1967), *The Voyage and Other Versions of Poems by Baudelaire* (1968), and *Notebook, 1967-68* (1969), have gone to insure the place he holds among living poets as well as to enlarge his image as a daring and original poet. *Notebook* is as radical a departure from *Life Studies* as that volume was from *Lord Weary's Castle.* Generally, in my collection I have tried to arrange the pieces, including the interviews, to follow the chronology of Lowell's published work and to suggest the many facets of his complex and extraordinary personality.

J.M.

Contents

1917   Robert Traill Spence Lowell, Jr., born on March 1, Boston, Massachusetts, the only child of Robert T. S. and Charlotte Winslow Lowell.

1924   Parents settle in Boston; the poet enters Brimmer School.

1930   Enters St. Mark's School. Classmates include Alfred Corning Clark and Frank Parker. Meets the poet Richard Eberhart.

1935-1937   Student at Harvard. Meets James Laughlin.

1937-1940   Meets Ford Madox Ford and Allen Tate. Transfers to Kenyon College where he studies with John Crowe Ransom and meets Randall Jarrell and Peter Taylor. Contributes to undergraduate magazine *Hika.*

1940   Enters Roman Catholic Church, marries Jean Stafford, and receives an A.B. *summa cum laude* in Classics from Kenyon College.

1940-1941   Teaches at Kenyon College.

1941-1942   Works as an Editorial Assistant for Sheed and Ward in New York City. Spends winter of 1942 with the Tates in Monteagle, Tennessee.

1943   Opposes Allied practice of saturation bombing; indicted for failure to report for draft induction; sentenced to one year and a day and released from prison after five months. Parole in Black Rock, Connecticut.

1944   Publishes *Land of Unlikeness.*

1946   Publishes *Lord Weary's Castle.*

1947   Pulitzer Prize for Poetry; Guggenheim Fellowship; Prize from American Academy of Arts and Letters; appointed Poetry Consultant to the Library of Congress.

1948   Divorced from Jean Stafford.

1949   Marries Elizabeth Hardwick; judge on committee awarding
            Bollingen Prize to Ezra Pound for *Pisan Cantos.*

1950   Father dies.

1950-1953   First trip to Europe.

1951   Publishes *The Mills of the Kavanaughs.*

1952   Harriet Monroe Prize.

1953-1954   Teaches at State University of Iowa.

1954   Mother dies; he returns to Boston.

1957   Daughter Harriet Winslow Lowell born.

1959   Publishes *Life Studies.*

1960   National Book Award for *Life Studies;* Guinness Poetry Award;
            Ford Foundation Grant to study opera; Longview Foundation
            Award. Participates in Boston Arts Festival. Moves to New York
            City.

1961   Publishes *Imitations* and *Phaedra.*

1962   Co-winner of Bollingen Prize for Translation. Visits South Amer-
            ica.

1964   Publishes *For the Union Dead; The Old Glory* (plays) produced by
            the American Place Theatre. Inducted into American Academy
            of Arts and Letters.

1965   Publishes *The Old Glory;* Obie Award for *Benito Cereno;* visits
            Egypt; declines invitation to White House Arts Festival because
            of the country's involvement in Vietnam.

1966   Loses Oxford Chair of Poetry election to Edmund Blunden.

1967   Publishes *Near the Ocean; Prometheus Bound* (play) produced at
            Yale.

1968   Publishes *The Voyage and Other Versions of Poems by Baude-
            laire.* Participates in the opening of the Olympic Games in
            Mexico City.

1969   Publishes *Prometheus Bound* and *Notebook, 1967-68.*

1970   Publishes expanded and revised *Notebook.* Teaches at University
            of Essex.

DeSales Standerwick

Notes on Robert Lowell

Beauty is practically indefinable, and readers of Robert Lowell's two volumes of poetry may have asked themselves, "Where is the beauty in the harsh turbulence of *Lord Weary's Castle?* How can the themes of incest and suicide in *Mills of the Kavanaughs* be termed 'beautiful'?" But beauty is there, and such readers should be persuaded to dip further, to reread, to ponder, in order to perceive it.

Few attempts have been made to get at the foundations of his poetry, what Lowell himself might call "the tap-root." The most satisfactory and inclusive work has been done by a poet one year older than Lowell, Randall Jarrell, in his *Poetry and the Age.* Mr. Jarrell sees in Lowell a dichotomy: the struggle between self and selflessness; between constriction and expansion; between cold and warmth; between evil and good; between Satan the Serpent and Christ. All that is good is to be found in Christ, "Lamb of the Shepherds," "the blue kingfisher," "Child of blood," "Jonas Messias," "wanderer and child," "the risen Jesus," "the Man-Fisher," "the sudden Bridegroom," "Is," "the dove of Jesus." In these epithets, some of which are hardly traditional, Lowell is coping with and overcoming the problem that faced T. S. Eliot and other poets who have attempted serious religious verse dealing with the spiritual crises of our times. Lowell's descriptions of the Christ Who will save "this ferris wheel" spinning in these "weak-kneed roots" are so in tune with the mood, imagery, and movement of his poems that there can be no shuddering at them.

Absolute, sweeping divisions in the poetry of Robert Lowell would be misleading because the poems often treat of several or all of Lowell's enigmas. For the sake of convenience one can divide Lowell's subject-matter into the sea, death, war, Boston and money, and religion, bearing in mind that often these are interfused. Of sea poems "The Quaker Graveyard at Nantucket" is

From *Renascence,* VIII (1955-56), 75-83. Reprinted by permission of the journal and Very Reverend Michael Daniel.

acknowledged to be his best. "At the Indian Killer's Grave" is about death. "Napoleon Crosses the Berezina" is a representative war poem. "As a Plane Tree by the Water" strikes against greed and landed-interests. "Where the Rainbow Ends" centers about Boston towards which Lowell's feelings are, to say the least, strange. On the subject of religion, which ordinarily brings to Lowell's mind Calvinism and Puritanism, "Mother Marie Therese" should be studied, a poem which has been compared to Hopkins' *Wreck of the Deutschland.*

"The Quaker Graveyard at Nantucket," a kind of elegy in memory of Warren Winslow, dead at sea, is divided into seven parts. The parts deal mostly with the cruel sea. The language is bitter and searing: the only exception is the sixth section entitled, "Our Lady of Walsingham," where the gentleness and ease of the words are appropriate to his subject.

It is night in a violent sea which throws up a drowned sailor who then is, not thrown back, but buried in the sea. The sea is powerful and has wrought its evils on the sailor who was "matted head and marble feet," nothing but a "botch of reds and whites." The serious tenor of the poem is enforced by the reference to fated Ahab's "void and forehead." The poet addresses the sailors who buried the corpse, and all sailors who have foolishly tried to "sand-bag this Atlantic bulwark"; when the sucking sea takes, it does not give back. Not even the lute of the Thracian Orpheus could make the Atlantic release its hold on the thousands of Eurydices it has taken unto itself.

The poet then brings us to shore where the winds coming in from the sea bespeak disaster, and tell us of a broken Pequod. The winds are birds whose "wings beat upon the stones," who "scream for you, Cousin," whose claws try to throttle the life out of the sea. In the Quaker graveyard where the poet is meditating, "the bones / Cry out . . . for the hurt beast," for the whale over which man was given dominion by the Lord God.

In the third part, there is again a direct address to the poet's cousin, Warren Winslow. Nothing we gain from the sea is of any avail or any value. There are some human powers, like guns, which can "roil the salt and sand"; but the sea lives with another time, the kind of time whose "contrition blues" and destroys and removes all traces of the havoc it has wrought. We may dream of the "castles in Spain," but the drowned learn only of the Ville d'Is, a city fabled to have been submerged because of the King's wicked daughter. The poet ends with the bitter irony of the poor Quakers relying on God's help while the very "monster's slick" carries them down to the depths of the sea.

Section four could well be an eloquent epilogue to *Moby Dick.* The end of "snatching at straws," of sailing the seas, hunting whales, fighting the unknown and the untameable, is only bitterness. We cry from the depths, says the poet, echoing the lament of King David in the Psalms. When the sea has done its full work, it leaves "only the death-rattle of the crabs." How like human life is this, the life of man fighting the sea; "we are poured out like water;" and King David had continued, "and all my bones are scattered." David had begun this terrible song of woe with the words immortalized later by a crucified Christ: "My God, my God, why hast thou forsaken me?"

The fifth part fills in a rather accurate description of a dismembered and decaying whale on the beach. It is said that there is nothing to equal the smell of a whale town where "the roll / Of its corruption overruns this world." In the pit of the dead, the decayed bones of the slain cry vengeance on the white whale, Moby Dick, and the sea that destroyed them. The whale fights on relentlessly till its dying gasp. Life struggles on, in man and beast; in man, the struggle is misdirected, so that the poet prays at the end, "Hide, / Our steel, Jonas Messias, in Thy side," a line complicated because of its allusions. We need a Saviour, Who is the Messias; and because of our interminable struggle against the white whale of evil, we call Him a Jonas Messias. As Jonas entered a whale's belly for three days and emerged safely, so our Messias and Saviour will enter the belly of the earth, the land of the dead, and in three days will emerge victorious and triumphant over life's most fearful event. Our steel that He hides in His side may well be the lance that will bring forth water and blood on Calvary, announcing the consummation of our Redemption.

It is here that the poet introduces a section seemingly foreign to the poem: "Our Lady of Walsingham." Not only is the locale changed from the New England coast to England, but it has its own title, and is an apostrophe to Mary, the Mother of the Redeemer, whose shrine at the Carmelite Monastery of Walsingham in Norfolk, England, had been the most popular shrine to Mary in pre-Reformation days until it was destroyed in the year 1538. The hard, bitter language is gone, the hopelessness of life is gone. "Shiloah's whirlpools gurgle and make glad / The Castle of God. Sailor, you were glad / And whistled Sion by that stream." The lines resemble Milton's introduction to *Paradise Lost:* "Or, if Sion hill / Delight thee more, and Siloa's brook that flowed / Fast by the oracle of God." The poet sees no beauty in the Shrine's statue of our Lady; he applies to Mary Isaias' words about the Messias: "There is no beauty in him, nor comeliness;" the new sorrow for Mary is, "Not Calvary's Cross nor crib at Bethlehem" but her dethronement from Walsingham and the heart of England. But the poet sees great hope that, not only England as once, but "the world shall come to Walsingham" to reap the fruits of the redemption and salvation wrought by "our steel, Jonas Messias, in Thy side."

This hope contrasts sharply and sadly with the ominous words of the last line in part seven. The Atlantic is once again invoked as destroyer and corrupter, "fouled with the blue sailors." If you could fathom mysterious depths of the sea, you would find yourself watching God in the act of creation, for the sea is the most elemental being in the universe. But even then, in the dawn of being, the "blue-lung'd combers lumbered to the kill." And the poet's musings upon this untamed monster make him say: "The Lord survives the rainbow of His will." The Book of Genesis relates how God made a covenant with Noe after the destructive flood: "I will set my bow in the clouds, and it shall be the sign of a covenant between me, and between the earth." The rainbow is the sign of hope and salvation; but if we do not fulfill our part of the covenant, the Lord will "render to every man according to his deeds." Thus the poem ends on a dire note with the threat that Ahab's fate may be our own if the monster overtakes us.

In "At the Indian Killer's Grave" the poet meditates upon death as he looks in King's Chapel Burying Ground where the first stone is marked 1658. In the last stanza he tells us that "I ponder on the railing at this park"; it is a down-sloping piece of burial ground, set in the middle of Boston, hemmed in by the street, the chapel, business blocks, and the city hall. He opens his meditation by saying that what is now left of the dead and their graves is a visible link from this world to the world of the spirit, to the great valley of Jehoshaphat where "I," the Lord, "will sit to judge all nations round about, . . . in the valley of destruction." Will things be reversed in that valley of true judgment? Will King Philip, great Indian chief of the slaughtered Wampanaogs, plait (get ready for the scalping?) the hair of these buried men, once considered heroic for their war against the Indians? "Friends" the poet calls these dead, who are so close to the roaring Boston subway. Death is an engraver, whose impressions are final and everlasting. (Could Lowell be punning on the word *engraver:* one who puts others into a grave?) These dead are forced by death to enter the dangerous valley and face the Lord's judgments.

This cemetery is not a pleasant spot, with its "dusty leaves and frizzled lilacs." So dreary is it that it seems as though the dust of the dead and the off-scourings of the town have blended. Charles II and England come upon the scene when in 1646, a petition praying for the privilege of Episcopal worship in King's Chapel was made to the King. Now "strangers hold the golden State House dome," for it used to be a common opinion that the Chapel Burying Ground contained only the bodies of Episcopalians. Among the remains the poet can see the tomb of John and Mary Winslow; John Winslow was the brother of Governor Edward Winslow; John's wife, Mary Chilton, was one of the *Mayflower* passengers. What is perhaps of more interest: Major Thomas is buried in this graveyard; he was one of the commanders in King Philip's War, and probably stands for the Indian Killer of whom Lowell speaks.

A subway train, envious perhaps of the dead, passes near. Changes come irrevocably; can the headstones marshal the dead to fight with the dragon that began its work in Genesis and continued straight through to the Apocalypse and beyond? In a terrifying picture, Lowell has the severed head of the Indian King Philip speak to the living. His head had in reality been cut off and hung in a prominent place to be mocked. The substance of his words is that the "Judgment is at hand"; that high-sounding and pretty speeches about religious election will not save the dead from the judgment. "The dead hand of time" is too relentless, too exacting.

Entering this man-hole (grave) you no longer give orders; you only receive. The surrounding buildings try to prevent the spread of the graveyard which is well-kept externally; but the mouse cracking walnuts by the headstones re-emphasizes what the graveyard is and is meant to be.

The last stanza is the most difficult one in the poem. The poet reflects on what he has seen. The men lying in the graves were possibly "fabulous or fancied patriarchs." They built a kingdom for their heirs, but sowed only dragon's teeth which would sprout up armed men to slay them. The poet then calls upon the four evangelists to take him to the Garden where Mary overcomes the Devil or dragon previously mentioned. The scene parallels somewhat the first half of the twelfth chapter of the Apocalypse in which the dragon fights the woman and her seed. Up to this point, the poem's attitude has been one of hostility and fear towards death; but when Christ the Bridegroom enters quickly, death is no more, for Christ has vanquished it.

Beneath the title, "Napoleon Crosses the Berezina," Lowell has inscribed Christ's words: "Wherever the body is, there will the eagles be gathered together" (*Matthew: 24,18*). Christ is here speaking of the Last Day. War is like the end of the world. All wars are alike; to express continuity, the poet depicts Napoleon as "Charlemagne's stunted shadow." Dreaming dreams, Napoleon marched into Russia, which will contain for him only "tombstone steppes." In 1812, Napoleon was retreating from Moscow; in November of that year, the Russian forces attacked him as he was crossing the Berezina River. Tremendous losses were inflicted upon the would-be conqueror. At that same river, in July, 1941, a fierce battle raged while the Germans were marching on Smolensk. Again, we get that sense of continuity of history. The poet calls upon the God of the "dragonish, unfathomed waters" to come up and wreak havoc on this war-monger. The river cannot chew up the bridges; but it is just as effectively changing them into tumbrils, the wicked, little carts that led the condemned Frenchmen to the guillotine during the Revolution. Add to the river the paralyzing snow and Napoleon's journey becomes truly "carrion-miles to Purgatory."

When war becomes a favorite pastime of leaders and nations, then really "we are poured out like water," we are wasted, we are condemned. It only remains for the eagles to hover over the place where the bodies shall be. Nor does Robert Lowell assuage the harsh tenor of his words, for war has stalked its prey too long and too doggedly.

The title of the poem "As a Plane Tree by the Water" is taken from the book of Ecclesiasticus. There are Biblical overtones throughout. "Darkness has called to darkness" comes from the Psalms; the Psalm's theme is nature's splendor proclaiming the glory of God, and the purity of God's Law. But the message is reversed in the poem; darkness here bespeaks a knowledge of evil in a land like the ancient Babel where wicked pride brought God's curse and the confusion of tongues. The new Babel is Boston, and money is the besetting evil. The cursed city is in "a land / Of preparation" dedicated to the Blessed Mother of God. As Walsingham had its Lady shrine, so Boston becomes Babylon, and Mary "Our Lady of Babylon." The city once was Mary's chosen place but now it is crusted with flies, symbols of decay. It once had been "the apple of your eye."

The theme continues in the second stanza in which the poet hits directly at the ideologies which dream of perfect worlds, "floating cities," "tomorrow's city to the sun." But the sun shines endlessly on Boston's streets that seem to lead their walkers straight to hell; "And therefore I was weary of my life, when I saw that all things under the sun are evil, and all vanity and vexation of spirit." That same sun shall act as a sword against those who have held back from observing the Lord's injunctions.

The image in the last stanza is complex. The flies, whose name has reechoed throughout the poem disastrously, try to strike from Boston across the sea, to the old country where money did not talk, but where "the eyes of Bernadette . . . saw Our Lady so squarely that / Her vision put out reason's eye." The darkness of Boston, engendered by too much planning and too much thinking, is helpless before the vision of this simple French girl. In the same way does Christ's victory over the tomb antagonize the people in the "floating cities" while it draws from the poet an ecstatic cry, "O walls of Jericho," as a symbol of the faith St. Paul speaks of: "By faith the walls of Jericho fell after they had gone around them for seven days." In contrast to the talking money of Boston, the faith of the Jewish people directed them to consecrate all the gold and silver of Jericho to the Lord. And with this supernatural faith, the very streets of the heavenly kingdom are "singing to our Atlantic wall" of the central and most important truth of Christianity: the Resurrection. But in Boston, things are the same: "Flies, flies are on the plane tree, on the streets."

The title of "Where the Rainbow Ends" is highly significative; Lowell used the rainbow in the "Quaker Graveyard at Nantucket." The rainbow again symbolizes God's hopeful covenant with man; but here, in a vision like St. John's in the Apocalypse ("I saw the holy city, New Jerusalem, coming down out of heaven from God"), the poet sees the end of the rainbow in Boston, and God's justice existing beyond it. The poem is full of epithets for cold, symbolizing constriction and narrowness, greed and selfishness, Satan and evil: "winters" "winter," "whistle at the cold." Extreme barrenness wastes the land; even the just are in danger, for "The worms will eat deadwood to the foot / Of Ararat" where Noe landed after the flood. "Time and Death" move in against the life of the spirit; Judaism and Christianity "are withered"; a bridge spanning the Charles River makes an idle mockery out of God's promising rainbow. "Dead leaves" abound. The poet considers himself, like St. John, "a red arrow on this graph / Of Revelations." The doves, once bought and sacrificed to appease the Almighty, are exhausted. The evil times have destroyed the glorious rainbow, and the powers of darkness exult in this satanic world. As he is a red arrow, so the poet is a victim who expects to die on "the thorn tree." He ascends the altar and sings the praises of Christ the lion, Christ the lamb, Christ the beast, Who stands before the throne of Him Who said to Moses: "I am Who am." Overawed by the "gold / And a fair cloth," and the "wings" of the "dove of Jesus" beating his cheeks, he feels disappointment and calls himself an exile, one in a place where he does not belong. But just as a dove brought an olive branch to Noe on Mount Ararat, so the dove of Jesus brings the victim "an olive branch" of peace and holiness "to eat." The reference is, of course, to Christ's Body and Blood. "Both the old covenant and the new still hold, nothing has changed: here as they were and will be—says the poem—are life and salvation."

The structure of this poem deserves special mention. Its three stanzas are constructed alike: ten lines each, with the rhyme scheme: *abcbcadeed*. Each line has ten syllables, save for the sixth which has six syllables; the rhymes are so arranged that only rereading discovers them.

A dramatic poem, "Mother Marie Therese," is spoken in couplets by an aged "Canadian nun stationed in New Brunswick." She is sitting before a fire, "piling on more driftwood," and she thinks of her Mother Superior who had been drowned. The Mother Superior, well beloved by her subjects, had been an elegant woman who had tried to reconcile her elegance with the Lord's command: "If thou wilt be perfect, go, sell what thou hast, and give to the poor, and thou shalt have treasure in heaven; and come, follow Me." But Mother Therese tried to straddle heaven and earth; the evil perhaps was not as great for herself as for the young sisters who felt "raptures for Mother." Mother's tastes were on the exquisite side: "strangled grouse / And snow-shoe rabbits;" "hounds;" "manor grounds;" "flowers and fowling pieces;" "Rabelais;"

"*Action Française,*" "Damascus shot-guns," "Hohenzollern emblems." She
tried to give her charges the impression that one could hold on to the things
of this world and still save one's soul.

But God chastised her; she fell sick and decided to renounce her belongings.
She only succeeded in half-renouncing them. Some time later, the Mother was
drowned on an excursion, and the good subject, many years later, sorrows
that the Mother had been deceived about life; or rather, that she had deceived
herself. Lowell magnificently describes the Mother's resting-place:

> The dead, the sea's dead, has her sorrows, hours
> On end to lie tossing to the east, cold,
> Without bedfellows, washed and bored and old,
> Bilged by her thoughts, and worked on by the worms,
> Until her fossil convent come to terms
> With the Atlantic.

The concluding lines are beautiful but enigmatic. The burden of his argument seems to be that the good sisters who realized that all was "false, false
and false," who feel sorrow when they recall "our young / Raptures for
Mother," are like the tormented soul in the *Hound of Heaven,* fleeing from a
God Who would bring them nothing but happiness. The sisters are "frost-
bitten," "ruinous," freezing; more than physical, this cold is spiritual, in the
soul. God is trying to master them but "we held our ears." "We must give
ground," they cry out, "but it does no good." The speaker feels the nearness
of Mother Therese trying to strengthen and enlighten her. But it is useless;
"My mother's hollow sockets fill with tears" not made from the swells of the
Atlantic.

Here again, the cold represents that constriction of the heart and soul that
produces unselfishness and egotism, that refusal to listen to the voice of God.
The speaker in the poem applies the evil universally, not only to the "snuf-
fling crones / And cretins" of the convent. "Our world that shams / His New
World, lost" is her condemnation of a civilization that is constricted through
and through.

Lowell's most ambitious work is his narrative poem, *The Mills of the
Kavanaughs,* which exhibits ease in its use of the open couplet. The narrative
elements are slim; Anne Kavanaugh, not of royal New England stock, thinks
about her blue-blooded husband who is dead. She relives certain events. After
his return from World War II, Harry Kavanaugh was ill. Listening to his wife
talking in her sleep, he came to the conclusion that she had been unfaithful to
him. Angered, he tried to choke, but doesn't harm her. The realization of

what she is increases the sickness in his mind until he tries to commit suicide, and finally ends up in an insane asylum where he dies.

The nightmares and dreams at times so interfuse with actual events and real memories that the direction the poet is taking seems vague and uncertain. The theme is again death and guilt and redemption. Death is too conclusive and exclusive: "Soon enough we saw / Death like Bourbon after Waterloo, / Who learning and forgetting nothing, knew / Nothing but ruin. Why must we mistreat / Ourselves with Death who takes the world on trust?" In fact, all the poems in this volume revolve around death. These poems have "a plaintive appealing, a calling to those who are gone—a reaching towards, a mild beseeching, out of the loneliness of life, of the dead husband, wife, mother and brother . . ."

My choice of Robert Lowell's poems is not meant to imply that the other poems are of less value or importance. Many of the others are outstanding, a few of which I can mention in passing. "In Memory of Arthur Winslow," an elegy for the poet's grandfather is the most cheerful poem on death that the poet has written. Though he castigates his grandfather for the "craft / That netted you a million dollars, late / Hosing out gold in Colorado's waste / Then lost it all in Boston real estate," he is confident that "the ghost / of risen Jesus walks upon the waves to run / Arthur" on to a new and better life. The last section is an impressive prayer to the Mother of God for his grandfather.

The two "Black Rock" poems are combinations of industrialization and redemption; of "Black Mud" which is a dragging body and a blue kingfisher, symbol of the redeeming Christ; of a world built of "defense-plants" and bent on "nightshifts" in the season of Christ's birth.

Some of the poems, like "The Death of the Sheriff," and "Her Dead Brother," deal with incest, a subject that Eugene O'Neill also associated with New England.

Lowell's departure from the Puritanism and Calvinism of New England has been sharp and complete. "Dunbarton" and "Children of Light" reveal a harshness that is not attractive. "They planted here the Serpent's seeds of light," he says; and, "Their sunken landmarks echo what our fathers preached."

There is little or nothing in the poetry of Robert Lowell to relieve the tension, either of a rasping, destructive nature, or of a blinded, deceived, and sinful race of men. The world in his eyes is an oceanic wasteland where the souls of men are tossed to and fro, violently and inexorably, till they must reach the depths of despair. Into this life already wasted and miserable comes greed; greed for land, which is imperialism; greed for money, which is capitalism; greed for power, which is war; greed for sex, which is incest and infidelity; greed for man-made religion, which is Puritanism; greed for one's self, which is suicide. All aching humanity, burning with greed and guilt and shame, is in tears for salvation that can come only through repentance; if it does not desire repentance, then the fires of hell and damnation must be evoked as a threat, for "the Lord survives the rainbow of His will."

Dudley Fitts

The Mills of the Kavanaughs

An *ad interim* book, maybe, but a fascinating one. It is as though this superlatively gifted poet, turning his back upon past excesses (which many, however, including myself, consider permanent triumphs of art), were feeling his way toward an austere and incompletely understood goal. As a result, these seven new poems are at once an enthralment and an exasperation: the first, because Robert Lowell could recast *Thirty Days Hath September* in terms that would tingle our scalps; the second, because so much technical virtuosity has been expended largely in chasing its own tail.

The form is dramatic monologue, Browning *viâ* Robinson; and the debt to both is constantly implied in diction, in phrasing, in the building of the verse paragraph. We have here an old man drowsing over his *Aeneid* when he should properly be at Sunday morning service in that white marvel of a Unitarian church in Concord. We have an hallucinated and very unhappy young widow dreaming of her childhood and marriage over a cheating game of solitaire. A Canadian nun remembering her dead Mother Superior. A Fat Man ("after Werfel"; I do not recognize the allusion) hilariously and tragically apostrophising himself in a mirror. And so on. These persons are as rounded, as alive, as Frà Lippo Lippi himself, or as Andrea. I suspect that I shall find them as unforgettable. And yet. . . .

I should like to dispose of "And yet" first. "And yet" is tortuosity. "And yet" is what the Spanish call *ripio,* padding the line. "And yet" is also a curious dereliction for which I can invent no better term than Inoperable Particularity.

From *Furioso,* VI (1951), 76-78. Reprinted by permission of the literary agent of the author's estate.

Let us see. "The Mills of the Kavanaughs," the title poem, is the one which I suppose the author would most willingly stand or fall by. It is a serious and beautiful poem; yet in my judgment it is gravely flawed. In the first place, its very form is over-demanding: it is cast in stanzas of sixteen riming lines—a worse clog to narrative (and this is, in effect, narrative reminiscence) than even the Spenserian stanza. The rimes ask too much, bring in too much; and, since Mr. Lowell is not economical in his handling, passage after passage sounds like a versification of the later prose of Henry James. To take an example from the first page:

> Our people had kept up their herring weirs,
> Their rum and logging grants two hundred years,
> When Cousin Franklin Pierce was President—
> Almost three hundred, Harry, when you sent
> His signed engraving sailing on your kite
> Above the gable, where your mother's light,
> A daylight bulb in tortoise talons, pipped
> The bull-mad june-bugs on the manuscript
> That she was typing to redeem our mills
> From Harding's taxes, and we lost our means
> Of drawing pulp and water from those hills
> Above the Saco, where our tenants drilled
> Abnaki partisans for Charles the First,
> And seated our Republicans, while Hearst
> And yellow paper fed the moose that swilled
> Our spawning ponds for weeds like spinach greens.

Claudite iam rivos, pueri: sat prata biberunt!, if I may appropriate a tag from one of Mr. Lowell's favorite poets. The greatest dunce in English A could easily riddle this stanza. Not only does it look, and read, like an entry for the Non-stop Sentence Derby: it is also dramatically false. A wife is addressing her dead husband. The facts are presumably as familiar to him as to her. But these facts must also be given to the reader, if he is to participate in the poem. Unhappily, they are not so much given to the reader as hurled at him: a fluid mélange of Charles I, William Randolph Hearst, President Pierce, bull-mad june-bugs and Bull (presumably Cousin Theodore's) Moose, President Harding, the Saco River, and the Abenaki Indians. And many of the details are not necessary to the poem: they seem to have been brought in to fill out the stanza; or else, to have been enforced by a kind of verbal association— thus, the name of Hearst inevitably produces the adjective "yellow." At any rate, the effect is one of turgidity verging upon the unreadable. And this stanza is not the exception, but almost the rule.

As for Inoperable Particularity: there is a great deal of it in the passage I have just quoted—the kind of detail that looks significant, that one worries about as a possible symbol, and that is finally rejected. For example (page 7):

> If her foot should slide
> a little earthward, Styx will hold her down
> *Nella miseria,* smashed to plaster, balled
> Into the whirlpool's boil.

Here everything is integral except the Italian tag: but are we really expected to add Paolo and Francesca to the already established Dis-Persephonê-Demeter theme? There seems to be no referent for *nella miseria*—no real excuse for it, except that it fits happily into the verse.

To my mind, the marvel is that out of a great deal of imperfectly assimilated history and one ancient bedroom joke Mr. Lowell has made, in "The Mills of the Kavanaughs," so moving a story. This girl in her garden, cheating at solitaire, laying open at every moment the darling cheapnesses and the unaware glories of human nature, touches me more than any woman I have encountered since the anonymous (and somehow similar) heroine of *The Statue and the Bust.* She is complete, and only an expert psychologist and dramatist could have created her. She is also deplorable, in the strict sense of the word; as deplorable, in the loose sense, as her language. And so it is with her co-agonists elsewhere in this book:

> Mother's great-aunt, who died when I was eight,
> Stands by our parlor sabre. 'Boy, it's late.
> Vergil must keep the Sabbath.' Eighty years,
> It all comes back. My Uncle Charles appears.
> Blue-capped and bird-like. Phillips Brooks and Grant
> Are frowning at his coffin, and my aunt,
> Hearing his colored volunteers parade
> Through Concord, laughs, and tells her English maid
> To clip his yellow nostril hairs, and fold
> His colors on him. . . .

If you want an example of the *flebile nescio quid,* it is in these lines. True, Charles Russell Lowell and Robert Gould Shaw seem to have got confused with one another, and the Boston purist may be forgiven for doubting if the Negro regiment ever *did* parade through Concord—but how rich, how evocative, the verses are! "Blue-capped and bird-like" is in itself a lesson in poetry, and the association of "colored volunteers" with the dead soldier's "colors" is masterly. Or, in a more deadly vein, the girl speaking in "Her Dead Brother":

> Then you were grown; I left you on your own.
> We will forget that August twenty-third,
> When Mother motored with the maids to Stowe,
> And the pale summer shades were drawn—so low
> No one could see us; no, nor catch your hissing word,
> As false as Cressid!

"The Mills of the Kavanaughs" is a more profound work, dramatically and emotionally, than "Falling Asleep Over the *Aeneid*" or "Her Dead Brother"; but there is a directness, a tension, in these minor poems that may prove to be the lasting value of this book. That it will last, I entertain no doubt: for once I can sincerely echo a dust jacket testimonial: "This," says John Berryman, "is a talent whose ceiling is invisible."

DeSales Standerwick

Pieces too Personal

This small volume [*Life Studies*], the first to issue from Robert Lowell in a long while, does not, in my opinion, match his remarkable achievement in either *Lord Weary's Castle* or *The Mills of the Kavanaughs*. This observation is strengthened by the presence in the book of a particularly well-written memoir entitled "91 Revere Street" that comes through to the reader with greater sharpness, clarity and spirit than many of the poems.

Part of the disappointment in the volume stems from the subject-matter of the poems. The majority of the poems are personal reflections on the poet's life—his childhood, grandparents, places associated with his life, his mother, his own illness and marriage and fatherhood. But so excellent is the writing in the prose memoir that these poems do not shine out with the same happy and careful expression of his observations. The universality of the experiences of human life, the piercing judgments on a deceptive way of living, the almost prophet-like vision of a gigantic mind—all present in the former volumes—do not appear in these poems that take for their starting points either very

From *Renascence*, XIII (1960), 53-56. Reprinted by permission of the journal and Very Rèverend Michael Daniel.

particular childhood memories or admired authors (Ford Madox Ford, George Santayana, Delmore Schwartz, Hart Crane), or individualized personifications ("The Mad Negro Soldier," "The Banker's Daugher," "To Speak of the Woe That Is in Marriage"). Somehow the author does not seem to get beyond the limited vision that enwraps the subject-matter of the various poems and to see the universal truth that might be present in the individual instance.

Lowell, of course, has his own idiom, and it is his manner of expression that made his former poems jump off the pages and dazzle the reader's eyes, the more so in that his use of rhyme was so expert, so exact, and most often unobtrusive. The memoir-poems in this volume are unrhymed; about five other poems have rhymes scattered through them; only seven are fully and somewhat intricately and artistically rhymed. His use of rhyme was an important quality of Lowell's poetry since it gave part of the beauty and music and unity to many of his former poems.

The same observation can be made about the imagery of the poems in the present collection. Formerly, the imagery was rich, exuberant, unique, yet always functional and more than likely tightly unified, giving the poems that rare quality of true vision granted the poet, and shared with the world around him.

The "family" poems in *Life Studies* lack this imagery save in rare instances: ". . . its alley of poplars/paraded from Grandmother's rose garden/to a scary stand of virgin pine . ."; "Distorting drops of water/pinpricked my face in the basin's mirror"; ". . . the clump of virgin pine still stretched patchy ostrich necks/ over the disused millpond's fragrantly woodstained water . . ."; "his thermos of shockless coffee. . ."; the captured newts lay dumb "as scrolls of candied grapefruit peel."

What these lines profess is a keen memory and a sharp eye for detail, being profuse in descriptions of houses, rooms, bric-a-brac, dress, stances and poses. Many of these descriptions are happily worded; it may be that these poems derive their universality in the accurate and quite honest portraitures they give of human beings—although, again, in their details and in their overall aspects, they could be more closely knit together and unified. I will take just a few of the poems for special comment.

The short poem, "For Sale," is a brief picture-poem in which the poet states that his father's cottage, possessed for only a year, had to be sold when the father died. His mother lingered in the house the day they were to leave. The cottage was a "sheepish" plaything; the furniture, out of place in the country, seemed to be waiting nervously for the moving men. His mother had the stupefied, dull look of a person who had failed to debark at the correct train station. The poet sympathizes with the cottage as if it had received a bad deal. His tone implies he condemns, not too seriously, the lavish wilfulness with which it has been outfitted. But what effects him most is the sight of his mother sitting abstractedly near a window, realizing that the disposal of the cottage is one more concrete evidence of her husband's death and absence. One is tempted almost to let his eyes skip from the title "For Sale" down to his words about his mother, as if he were making some mental connection between the two.

The poem, "For George Santayana," sympathetic in tone and outlook, seems to be the result of a personal visit to the Catholic monastery where George Santayana spent the last years of his life. It opens with a description of what has now become the typical European viewpoint of Americans as "souvenir deranged" until it speaks directly to Santayana, calling him that "stray spirit, who'd found/the Church too good to be believed," although "the world too prosaic to be lived in" might more accurately describe the straying, aloof attitude of Santayana.

As in so many of his poems, Lowell continues here that bridging of history that establishes his ideas and moods with the tradition that has gone before. The Roman and Greek worlds creep in with the references to the Circus and the Mithraic Temple, lying as they do on his way to Santo Stefano, representing the Christian Rome; in any event, Roman or Christian, old or modern, it is to him "Bella Roma," as he avers in the poem, "Beyond the Alps." The world of philosophical thought, so dear to Santayana though he appears to have been so individualistic in his approach and development, is present in the references to Socrates and Alcibiades.

The poems in this volume are not heavily laden with the imagery that we usually associate with the sensitive and fanciful mind of a poet. This to me is a weakness in the writing, especially in the remembrance poems. In the Santayana poem, the conclusion does contain this magic of imagery, and presents a fine word-picture of the aged philosopher:

> near ninety,
> still unbelieving, unconfessed and unreceived,
> true to your boyish shyness of the Bride.
> Old trooper, I see your child's red crayon pass,
> bleeding deletions on the galleys you hold
> under your throbbing magnifying glass,
> that worn arena, where the whirling sand
> and broken-hearted lions lick your hand
> refined by bile as yellow as a lump of gold.

There are in this collection six sonnets, if we include the three that loosely make up the poem, "Beyond the Alps." The three single sonnets differ in subject-matter (marriage, Hart Crane, Inauguration Day) as well as in rhyme scheme and meter. In this former poetry Lowell used the two-line rhyme in as masterful a fashion as possible. In this volume he has abandoned it save in occasional places, as in the sonnet, "To Speak of Woe That Is in Marriage." Also in his earlier work, Lowell was almost scrupulous in his use of a quasi-poetic diction. Now he resorts to expressions like "dope or screw" (as nouns), "hopped up husband," "screwball" and "Mayflower screwballs." True, in context these are from monologues spoken by types or particular people; still, his imagination used to be able to come up with words more exact and more poetic.

The sonnet, "Words for Hart Crane," puts into the mouth of Crane harsh words the tragic poet might speak to some "stranger in America." The poem is earthy and hard, using slang prose like "phoney gold-plated laurels" and "wolfing the stray lambs." It catches the literary ranking of Crane by references to Whitman (who had great influence on Crane), to Catullus, and to Shelley. The fourteen lines are as succinct and accurate a biography of this misguided genius as could be found, although omitting any mention of Crane's alcoholism. The problem of a man's free will might possibly be seen in, "I . . . used to play my role/of homosexual," as if a human being, plagued by perverse and not so latent desires, had to become their slave; as though that were the role assigned to him in life and he had no choice but to play it. The last two lines preserve the poem from becoming too strident and harsh an indictment of American literature's neglect of Crane, whose work gains greater stature as the years pass.

Life Studies also contains a thirty-five page memoir of Lowell's earlier life, memories that "hover . . . in recollection," where "The things and their owners come back urgent with life and meaning." Somehow, there is little of Robert Lowell or his doings in these memoirs; rather, they are a small boy's reflections, gathered and matured in retrospect, upon his "forlornly fatherless" father, and his haughty and chilly mother; upon his home at 91 Revere Street, which acts as the focal point for his launching out into the world of education; upon the Sunday dinners and visitors, naval and otherwise, at Revere Street; upon the "rocklike" things—Major Mordecai Myers' portrait in the forefront—connected with the house and fastened securely in his memory. It is the type of rambling, loose memoir that I personally feel every adult should write for himself so that he might preserve and clarify those conscious impressions of what his childhood and home life were.

Not everyone's prose would have the pungency and kick and open honesty of Lowell's writing. Nor would they be so blessed as to be surrounded by phrase-makers and quotable talkers. Lowell's mother is by far the best. She spoke of the family receiving some trust-fund money "not grand enough to corrupt us but sufficient to prevent Daddy from being entirely at the mercy of his salary." Other memorable comments include: "We are barely perched on the outer rim of the hub of decency"; "Alone and at night an amateur driver is unsafe in a car"; "Your inebriated sailors have littered my doorstep with the dregs of Scollay Square"; "I have always believed carving [of dinner roasts] to be *the* gentlemanly talent." Captain Atkinson was in her displeasure because he was "unable to tell one woman from another." The whole of this essay is delightful, truthful (we presume), warm-hearted and memorable.

If I have been too harsh in my judgment on these latest Lowell poems, it is because my disappointment arises from a comparison of those works with his former poems. There are, be it known, many excellent passages in the poems—incisive phrases, clear pictures, a diction for the most part unique, yet spontaneous. The stamp of an original writer is upon these lines. The difficulty, I think, comes from the subject-matter, which is often extremely personal, sometimes embarrassing, and occasionally too unique to be universalized.

Charles Altieri

Poetry in a Prose World: Robert Lowell's *Life Studies*

In his treatment of Robert Lowell's *Life Studies,* M. L. Rosenthal convincingly demonstrates that Lowell's confessional mode is not mere therapy but a powerful means for reaching and universalizing significant contemporary experience. He suggests that Lowell manages to transcend the personal largely by adapting his material to the modern tradition of the sequence poem, by relating the poems to one another, and by creating in the volume as a whole a context that deepens and objectifies the individual poems.[1] Yet, while Rosenthal shows how the poems are linked in style and subject, he does

---

From *Modern Poetry Studies,* I (1970), 182-99. Reprinted by permission of the journal.

[1] *The New Poets* (New York, 1967), p. 20, pp. 25-66 passim. For this essay I have used the following abbreviations: LS, *Life Studies* (New York, 1959); O, "Skunk Hour" in Anthony Ostroff's *The Contemporary Poet as Artist and Critic* (Boston, 1964); PR, "Interview," *Writers at Work: The Paris Review Interviews, Second Series* (New York, 1965); PG, "Prose Genius in Verse," *Kenyon Review,* XV (1953); AT, "A Talk with Robert Lowell," *Encounter,* XXIV (1965); RL, "Robert Lowell in Conversation with A. Alvarez," *The Review,* No. 8 (August 1963).

not consider at any length the thematic dynamism that informs these connections, gives them dramatic depth, and controls a complex set of interlock-
ing motifs. This dynamism gives to the volume its particular richness and adds
to its emotional impact. "Beyond the Alps," which opens the book, begins
the process. The poem's journey establishes the anxieties characteristic of
sequence poems like *Song of Myself,* the *Cantos,* "Comedian as the Letter C,"
Paterson, and *Homage to Mistress Bradstreet* as well as provides a key to the
book's overall unity. By a series of oppositions, it identifies Lowell's particular quest as a search for new secular values to replace Western culture's dying
traditions.

On the one side, "Beyond the Alps" indicates, are Rome, altitude, secular
and religious authorities, Church dogma and the heroic Classical world; on the
other, Paris breaking up, earth, landscape, and "pure prose." In short, the
oppositions exist between the fictive or mythic world of imagination and the
empirical world of fact. The old values have become fictions which no longer
meet the test of fact or keep off what Wallace Stevens called "the pressure of
reality." Mussolini is not the reincarnation of an Imperial Rome but "one of
us / only, pure prose"; the Pope's devotional candles are offset by his purring
electric razor. Even Paris, the city of art, which might restore a Hellas or a
viable paganism to replace Rome's authority, cannot do so, for it, too, is
breaking up. Man's dream of conquering mountains has not prevailed, and the
train must "come to earth" for Lowell to begin the search anew. The suggestion that "Life changed to landscape" could "serve as an epigraph for
the volume as a whole" conveys how the oppositions work.[2] The line
summarizes the dichotomy between vertical and horizontal that is basic
to the volume. A purely secular landscape has no objective center of
meaning, defines no values not chosen by the painter. It reveals no
hierarchy, nothing valuable in itself. Its horizontality opposes both the
typologies of Christianity and the symbolism of Romanticism where specific
objects and actions take on sacred or privileged existences.

---

[2] Jerome Mazzaro, *The Poetic Themes of Robert Lowell* (Ann Arbor, 1965), p. 90. In
some versions of the poem (see *For the Union Dead*), the line reads, "Man changed to
landscape." Mazzaro also points out the motif of animal imagery and connects it with
the problem of finding secular values, but my specific focus on the theme of secular
values leads me to reject his claims for corollary stresses on Poundian culture and secular
immortality. Hugh Staples has a relevant reading of "Beyond the Alps" in *Robert
Lowell: The First Twenty Years* (New York, 1962), p. 72. He points out that the poem's
journey establishes a metaphor that includes many other transitions in the volume and
concludes in "Skunk Hour." Irvin Ehrenpreis makes several interesting comments on the
differing functions of Rome and Paris in the poem in "The Age of Lowell," *Robert
Lowell: A Collection of Critical Essays,* ed. Thomas Parkinson (Englewood Cliffs, 1968).
Lowell elaborates on an opposition of Alpine and prosaic worlds in the opening
paragraphs of "I. A. Richards as a Poet," *Encounter,* XIV (February 1960), 77-78.

The equation of this horizontal realm with prose and earth prompts a new perspective on the symbolic effects of crossing the Alps, for, as the empirical world view gradually becomes dominant, prose gains in importance. This progress is apparent if we compare the novel with the epic it replaced. In all great epics, a vertical force—fate or destiny or the gods—invests the actions with significance and creates the values defining noble conduct. In the novel, on the other hand, action and value tend to be defined horizontally, by the flux of history, by the sociological conditions of the novel world, and by the interactions of the characters.[3] If we keep in mind the historical and epistemological affinities shared by the novel and the social sciences, we see the kind of naturalistic world in which Lowell's quest must work itself out. His task is to accept the empirical reductions of the old values to mere fictions, but not to stop there. He must suffer the pains of a naturalistic world—hence the volume's pervasive animal images and Lowell's stress on the past as the field of quest; but he must, at the same time, through pain transform the landscape by finding that secular basis for value that will make endurance possible. Lowell expresses this most succinctly in a review of *Brother to Dragons* where he speculates on poetry's need to reabsorb the prose world: "Eternal providence has warned us that our world lies all before us and nowhere else. Only the fissured atoms which destroyed Hiroshima and Nagasaki can build our new Atlantis" (PG, 120). Lowell's "new Atlantis" (the image is Plato's) will retain most of the old Humanistic values, but now the values will be secularly grounded. Ideally poetry will emerge through the poet's encounter with the prose world. In fact, Lowell calls these poems in *Life Studies* seeking the New Atlantis "more religious than the early ones" (PR, 352).

The quest for values in the prose world also informs the style of the volume. Most obviously it sustains the shift from Lowell's earlier "symbolic" or typological style where vertical meanings largely absorbed the concrete world to his new experience-centered manner.[4] What is less evident is the way the

---

[3] This view of the novel is supported both by Ian Watt's famous *Rise of the Novel* and by J. Hillis Miller, *The Form of Victorian Fiction* (South Bend, 1968), who stresses the horizontal nature of the novel world as a Victorian phenomenon arising from the death of God. However the contrast between *Paradise Lost* and say Defoe's work, a contrast pointed out to me by my colleague Roy Roussel, makes us locate at least the roots of Miller's description of the novel in the very beginnings of the form.

[4] The best treatment of Lowell's early style is contained in Jerome Mazzaro, "Robert Lowell and The Kavanaugh Collapse," *University of Windsor Review*, V (Fall 1969), 1-24. Lowell's own comments on *Life Studies* stress his move from a symbolic to an experience-oriented style and equate this new style with prose and with a reliance on the secular world. In the *Paris Review* Interview, he discusses the novel as "The ideal modern form" (PR, 343) and claims that prose is freer from rhetoric than poetry and closer to experience and vitality (PR, 345-46). In his essay on "Skunk Hour" and again in an interview with Alvarez, he talks about the prose of Flaubert, and especially of Chekhov, as models for his new style (O, 108; RL, 36). Some of the terms for this paragraph also derive from Frank Kermode, *The Sense of An Ending* (New York, 1967), pp. 133-150.

structures of *Life Studies* conform to this quest. As Angus Fletcher indicates in *Allegory* (1964), works constructed from a vertical perspective tend toward allegory; obvious patterns or paradigms control the subject matter. The clearcut interplay of levels (Dante) or the use of dramatic foils (Sophocles) communicates confidence in the fictional structure the mind possesses for grasping reality. In the horizontal world, typified by the modern novel, these forms seem no longer adequate or clear. Contingency becomes important. The paradigms or thematic organization of events no longer seem as capable of explaining events. Still, the reader, and usually the protagonist, require some recurrence in order to interpret the flux of reality and act purposively within it. The poems must not be mere records of experience. They must contain actions and qualities which are similar enough to allow some generalization, while at the same time being subtle enough not to call attention to that similarity. The mind must derive these meaningful relationships just as it would work in a horizontal world. Casual events, dictated by chance and corresponding to no preexistent pattern, must set up conditions where generalizations become problematic: what the mind seeks to bring together seems always to resist, to assert its own inviolable uniqueness. As Robert Creeley puts it in *Pieces* (1969): "Make time / of irritations, / looking for the / recurrence."

We can readily observe this change from vertical to horizontal styles if we compare typical poems from *Lord Weary's Castle* (1946) and *Life Studies.* In *Lord Weary's Castle,* the vertical, allegorical world manifests itself in two ways: in the typological and tightly repetitious use of motifs and in the tendency for Christ to enter the poems at the end, support Lowell's criticisms of the existing order, and provide a resolution. In other words, Christ is a privileged point of reference (possible only in a world that accepts an idea of grace), who gathers into himself the random events of the poem and both allows and sustains their interpretation. "Colloquy in Black Rock" illustrates the method. Its predominant motif is the horror of mud as an image for the all-leveling naturalistic world whose final conquest is the "mud-flat detritus of death." Less evident are the typological relationships of suffering, martyrdom, and building the Church. Lowell and the workers labor each in his own way, and assume meaning through protomartyr Stephen, who dies in order to build Christ's church. The poem ends in the resolving figure of Christ, the diving Kingfisher, who appears in a destroying, but ultimately purifying fire. He conquers the black mud of death and creates an order that redeems suffering. This conquest comes only through suffering and death, and, by its alliance with Stephen's, Lowell can feel his own suffering given meaning.

In *Life Studies,* "My Last Afternoon with Uncle Devereux Winslow" also concludes with the evocation of a dominant figure, but one which no longer absorbs directly the poem's other figures and motifs or represents a satisfactory resolution to the poem's tensions. Devereux is secular and more transformed by the world than transforming it. The difference between Christ's mastery and his powerlessness prompts the poem's different organizations. The stress on fusing verbal and linguistic patterns is gone. Now Lowell strives for syntactic and narrative casualness, a fidelity to the flux of experience that makes the poem appear spontaneous reflection and not artifact. Even when organizing patterns of repetition are perceived, they resist being formed into a general interpretative statement. The elements of these patterns adhere to specific contexts and relate only tangentially to other sections of the poem, whereas in the earlier poem the elements existed in order to be pulled together. Let me be specific. Motifs like water, the colors black and white, and echoes of the opposition of Alpine and ground level of "Beyond the Alps" run through "My Last Afternoon," but never so clearly coming into a summary that one can comfortably explore for their significance. Each section of the poem presents some form of death and frustration;[5] all, to evoke the decay of the tradition, refer to various kinds of art. In fact, the power of these objects to assume meaning inversely relates to their traditional hierarchic status: "Olympian perfection," music, and Greek statues lead to frustration, while "the works of my Grandfather's hands" and the mock-heroic pictures at Devereux's camp retain some vital family significance. The combination of these themes of death and frustration into the final artistic image of the heroically clothed Devereux pulls nothing together. Instead it complicates the relation of the previous images and Lowell's awareness of his heritage with its mixture of heroic and mock-heroic elements.

The construction of the volume *Life Studies* follows closely that of the poem, "My Last Afternoon with Uncle Devereux Winslow." Four sets of parallels, or casually developed motifs, seem basic: recurrent animal images, repeated references to lost father figures, presentations of different journeys, and, finally, secular versions of religious ritual—especially of Communion. Each motif begins by exploring the implications of lost values in a prose world and gradually evolves into a vision of the possibility of reconstituting some fundamental values. In Part I, Lowell puts into historical perspective the decline of the mythic imagination that sustained the vertical world. Figures of lost authority diminish into the degraded protagonist of "A Mad Negro Soldier Confined at Munich," the volume's first avatar. The process starts with the impossibility in "Beyond the Alps" of accepting religious and secular father figures. In "The Banker's Daughter" the decline continues. The

---

[5] Thus in the first section Lowell's parents' dreams are frustrated and at the end the pastoral world of the farm is shattered by a sudden reference to death; the second and third sections are marked by ironic frustrations of the Lowell wealth and culture; and the final section presents the ultimate frustration of life, of the power of the Lowells, and of the illusions of power and beauty.

King is reduced by the banker's daughter as devotion to Mary reduces the Pope. She represents the new utilitarian spirit which eventually destroys both monarchy and the Catholic Church. The implications of this reduction are sharply stated in the poem's concluding lines: "If you ever took / unfair advantages by right of birth, / pardon the easy virtues of the earth." In contrast to the old vices, the new suggest a surrender to the venal instincts and an acceptance of man's natural vulgarity rather than a humanistic attempt to transform it. Levelling all distinctions to "the easy virtues of the earth" prefigures ironically the levelling death which blends all "to the one color" (LS, 64).

"Inauguration Day: 1953" shows the culmination of the processes begun by "The Banker's Daughter." Ike is the father figure so reduced, so without the dignity of Hellas' altitude, that he can in no way stimulate the imagination or serve as a model for action. There is no relief, no promise in the demonic winter world of the poem. Prose world and earth have conquered: we are reduced to "cyclonic zero of the word." When this poem, too, comes around to death, death has become the spiritual condition of the living ("mausoleum in her heart").[6] "A Mad Negro Soldier Confined at Munich" carries the volume's levelling to a sensitive individual. In many respects it is as important structurally as "Beyond the Alps," for it introduces a figure who anticipates Lowell's handling of his own breakdown while its opening line, "We are all Americans," connects the breakdown to the preceding poem and its imaginative models.

As a precursor of Lowell's condition, "A Mad Negro Soldier Confined at Munich" adds to the pattern of animal imagery several motifs to be developed later in the volume and resolved eventually in "Skunk Hour"—the secular ritual of eating and the problem of passive surrender to one's plight. The soldier is completely mired in the prose world, incapable of asserting his human dignity. His speech treats human actions constantly in animal terms ("cat-houses," "cold-turkey," "chickens"), and at the poem's conclusion he equates his madness both with the subhuman animal condition and with his own blackness, a color that recalls the contrasts of "Beyond the Alps": "It's time for feeding. Each subnormal boot- / black heart is pulsing to its ant-egg dole." The figure finds no ritual significance in a meal. In fact, the meal is a "feeding," an animal activity. Because of this sense of subnormality, the speaker takes no responsibility for his situation. He submits passively to receiving "doles." In addition, the poem's opening line mention of America prefigures the explicit emphases of the problems of being an American in "Words for Hart Crane" and "Memories of West Street and Lepke," the two

---

[6]The last line can refer grammatically to both Ike and the Republic as a whole. Mazzaro points out that even details in the poem like the reference to Stuyvesant and Grant further portray the declining traditions (p. 95). Again they are potential figures of authority.

other poems presenting extreme examples of people in a world of "lost connections" (LS, 85).

In Part II, the problem of finding satisfactory cultural father figures throws Lowell back into his personal life and, in so doing, intensifies the importance of his father's failure to provide an imaginative model. The problem he confronts in the book's final section stems from the Commander's being a "prose" father, a biological relation who never becomes a human one: "I was a churlish, disloyal, romantic boy, and quite without hero worship for my father, whose actuality seemed so inferior to the photographs in uniform he once mailed to us from the Golden Gate. My real love, as Mother used to insist to all new visitors, was toy soldiers" (LS, 13). Three kinds of fathers emerge as relevant to the failure and to the vertical and horizontal creation of values. The first is God the Father, the ideal father, who completely determines both the son's essence and his courses of action. Classical literature provides a second, totally human father who transmits to his son both a sense of dignity and an ethical code. In the epic, for example, the heroic father is inextricably united with both the son's sense of value and his involvement in an acceptable tradition. In the twentieth century, however, we have neither Aeneas or Odysseus but Simon Dedalus and Commander Lowell. This difference goes a long way toward explaining the anguish, alienation, and frequent despair of the modern hero, who so often shares the feeling Lowell captures poignantly in the closing comment of section II, "I know why Young Bob is an only child."[7]

The danger in the father's failure to provide an adequate imaginative model is that a void may develop in precisely those areas where a father should mediate his son's entry into society and into the flux of experience. It is this void which Lowell is trying to fill through *Life Studies,* revealing in the prose description of his childhood the inauthentic stratagems he tends to substitute for other, more mature ways of coming to terms with problems of one's identity. First, to gain a sense of importance and individuality, the young Robert resorts to the acts of cruelty which demean Eric Burckhard, and later, as husband, to the cruel acts of " 'To Speak of Woe That Is in Marriage.' " Second, he develops a tendency to flee from responsibility—in part because his father is always the passive victim of others' intentions, and in part because he attributes a good deal of his father's failure to being always burdened by responsibilities, and hence, lacking the freedom to explode and assert at least some kind of emotional intensity, some claim to dignity (LS, 28).

---

[7]The consummate ironic skill of the prose section is quite evident here. For even this act of defining the nature of the son comes not from Commander Lowell but from the more vulgar Billy Harkness who has helped emasculate him. And the preference for toy soldiers over Commander Lowell is a brilliant touch.

The desire to escape responsibility first manifests itself in Charlotte Lowell's trying to force Robert to become the man of the house. He insists, "I am not a man, I am a boy" (LS, 24); he wants to retain a status that allows "outlawry and weakness" (LS, 25). Similar desires lead to his request to remain in a girls' school (LS, 30) and to his pleasure in being able to play the paramour when protected by the strong character of his grandfather (LS, 67). Thus, when first faced with adult responsibility as he realizes that grandfather's farm is now his, he immediately reverts to the two basic evasions of his childhood (LS, 68-69); he calls grandfather back to hold him as paramour ("have me, hold me, cherish me,"), and he revels in the gesture of doodling mustaches on the last Russian Czar (a continuation of the demythologizing of father figures, but here symbolically tied to Lowell's rejection of a possible father role for himself). The full impact of the theme of responsibility, however, comes only with Lowell's breakdown, for this ultimate rejection of responsibility returns him to the female passivity of his father and his father's fantasies. The breakdown provides the turning point in the volume, dramatically broaching these themes of maturity and responsibility.

In addition, two elements which are paramount in the emasculation of his father in the prose section fit into basic motifs in the book, as if the son must conquer those things which defeated his father before he can claim the dignity his father lacked. We notice first that the scenes Robert remembers most vividly as degradations cluster about meals, especially ritual meals. Admiral de Stael first calls Commander Lowell to leave home and sleep at the naval base while the family is gathered for Christmas Eve dinner (LS, 23) and Billy Harkness and the other naval men are usually guests for Sunday dinner. Secondly, Commander Lowell's two major antagonists, Charlotte and Billy Harkness, accomplish their degradations by distorting language. Billy degrades by his utter vulgarity, a vulgarity expressed in his jokes and in his refusal ever to be serious (Lowell often gives direct quotations from Billy and first characterizes him by quoting a bad joke, LS, 32). Charlotte's distortion of language is worse because half-deliberate: she hides her domination by her habit of "asking questions for the purpose of giving, not of receiving instruction" (LS, 27). (Yet the emptiest use of language remains for Commander Lowell who, thinking church beneath the dignity of a naval man, spends his Sunday morning lettering his initials on garbage cans, LS, 32.)

Lowell fully develops the contrast between the failings of his parents and his own quest to transcend them in the family section of *Life Studies*. These poems continue to strip away the dead fiction, but they develop basic motifs in such a way that his parents' empty actions are contrasted with his own more noble ones. This process is exemplified in the last lines of "Terminal Days at Beverly Farms." Here, the most horrifying aspect is Commander Lowell's inability to change, to adapt his naval habits to the civilian world he has entered. In contrast to those daily journeys to preserve pathetic fictions and acts of naming about as relevant as a Swiss navy, his son sees himself on a contradictory journey (through Switzerland) away from inoperable fictions and empty names. In addition, the father's fictions serve to deny reality by symbolizing it as something else—not by metonymy but by inauthentic metaphor. Such fictions require only the physical vision he is so proud of and, moreover, provide him no manly way of facing death, the undisguisable reality of the prose world. Thus his last words to his wife are really pathetic— a vague, passive surrender: "After a morning of anxious, repetitive smiling / His last words to Mother were: / 'I feel awful.' "[8] Even worse, they are the complaint of a sick child; they embody the commander's emasculation and surrender to the domination of his wife.

Part III of *Life Studies* investigates another kind of model—perhaps the only viable human model for Lowell. He turns to four modern artists, all only children in their own way, and finds a possible path of action, but one demanding great suffering. Since this entire sequence exists against a backdrop of empty social and artistic traditions, the specific individual quest, more than the work of the artist, becomes important to Lowell. In the two poems on prose writers, Ford Madox Ford's allegiance to empty tradition, to the idea of the art novel, leads to his demise (dying "in want") and sets off the more successful quest of George Santayana. Santayana remains completely in the prose world: like Lowell, he finds the fictions of Christianity "too good to be believed," and he even refuses the secular idealism of Socrates. Ideas are not the final test of philosophy; one must comprehend the violent, the unusual, and the chaotic—the world of "manslaying Alcibiades." To define Santayana's quest, Lowell turns to a religious figure: Santayana is both Daniel in the Lions' Den and the Christian martyr, entering the Colosseum of flux with only his language and his dedication as weapons:[9]

---

[8]Lowell draws a similar contrast between his own quest and the emptiness of his mother's life. For her, secular ritual becomes pure parody: "Mother, new/caps on all her teeth, was born anew/at forty" (LS, 71). And she too has her journeys. In "Sailing Home From Rapallo," symbols of the Risorgimento become on her casket closely allied with modern packaging devices like preservative tinfoil. In "For Sale," the notion of journey is evoked by an unheroic simile:

> Ready, afraid
> of living alone till eighty,
> Mother mooned in a window
> as if she had stayed on a train
> one stop past her destination.

She becomes another figure rendered passive and lost in the void created by the rush of the modern world. Without inner strength, she can only face death passively and "in want" (LS, 50).

[9]Santayana is the real "trooper" (the wielder of Grandfather's cane, not Commander Lowell's putter). While Ford fictionalizes war, Santayana really becomes the good soldier in a more important battle.

> Old trooper, I see your child's red crayon pass,
> bleeding deletions on the galleys you hold
> under your throbbing magnifying glass,
> that worn arena, where the whirling sand
> and broken-hearted lions lick your hand
> refined by bile as yellow as a lump of gold.

A similar secularized rite concludes "To Delmore Schwartz." The poem explicitly connects Lowell with the volume's universal *Angst,* and the misquotation of Wordsworth provides an ironic comment on the way poetry can define our condition, "We poets in our youth begin in sadness;/thereof in the end come despondency and madness." But the human fellowship of the last lines offers momentary relief from despair:

> we struck
> the duck
> 's web-
> foot, like a candle, in a quart of gin we'd killed.

The simile, echoing the Pope's devotional candles, transforms the drunken scene into a parody of the communion ritual: the poets preside at a horizontal, non-sacramental celebration of the lines and by the brilliant word "killed" which explodes the cliché to suggest the desperation behind the ritual. The poets really are engaged in a kind of desperate battle to get drunk. The desperation which creates fellowship leads naturally into "Words For Hart Crane" where Lowell's sense of what it entails to become a poet who can meet and transform the prose world lets him define Crane's quest in terms that lead naturally into the confessional section of the volume, "Who asks for me, the Shelley of my age,/ must lay his heart out for my bed and board."

The Crane poem is especially important not only because it so clearly defines the horror of the quest Lowell must undergo but also because the method of the poem suggests how poetry can be a redeeming secular agent. Lowell has not yet shown his own sufferings, so he makes this dramatic monologue a new kind. Traditionally, the dramatic monologue stresses the independence of the fictive speaker; the externalization of his fictive character is essential to the poet's purposes and creates a distance that allows analysis and an ironic perspective. Here, though, as the title indicates, Lowell wants to internalize the speaker. He wants to deny the fictiveness of the poem or, at least, to use that fictiveness as a means for involving himself in another's actual existence. The denial is part of a requirement in *Life Studies* that the models both enable Lowell to identify his own suffering and provide him a solution to be imitated. In denying the usual aesthetic distance of dramatic monologue, Lowell also denies some of the emptiness present in "To Delmore Schwartz."

Lowell's own attempt to get "at the center of things," to explore fully after his own breakdown, the horrors of a horizontal world, away from his parents' failures and in terms of the artist as his only viable human model, leads to "Waking in the Blue," the poem best expressing his degradation. We have again the demonic winter landscape of "Inauguration Day: January 1953" and the plethora of animal images ("seal," "cock," "thoroughbred") recalling the wolves and lambs of Hart Crane and the images in "A Mad Negro Soldier Confined at Munich." In addition, McLean's, a private rest home outside of Boston, contains the perversion of all possible secular salvations: an "azure" day creates only bleakness inside; a Harvard education produces only Stanley thinking of his body and "more cut off from words than a seal"; the French king reappears as a naked and insane replica of Louis XVI; and, finally, the future only repeats the present, "These victorious figures of bravado ossified young." This inversion of normality rounds out the last stanza. Its illusions of healthy, almost heroic actions shatter on reaching the "metal shaving mirror."

The casual shift here makes us aware of the terrifying inversion of normal life that madness is. The common elements usually so taken for granted become potential instruments of violence or suicide. The choice of mirror as the specific focus for the shift intensifies the horror because the mirror, like art, is a way of defining the self, of assuring some coincidence between inner and outer self. To see oneself in a metal mirror is to reverse this normal assurance, to receive in the attempt to grasp the self a reminder of the potential tenuousness of that existence. The poem then makes explicit for Lowell his real fears. He too might become "ossified" like the others into a too "familiar" future, a future whose horror is suggested by the last inversion of normal life—the locked razor.

Lowell's plight in "Waking in the Blue" gives great significance to "Home After Three Months Away" where the possibility of a purely secular redemption of his suffering is suggested. The suggestion is contained in the readaptation of the shaving ceremony to normal domestic circumstances. Shaving becomes an act which he shares with his daughter: it holds together and is held together by the family structure. Their love for one another allows a new perspective on animal images. When Lowell tells his daughter, "Dearest, I cannot loiter here/in lather like a polar bear," he humanizes the purely naturalistic being that animal images had suggested previously. He can now allow himself a humorous, lightly ironic point of view in a language whose precision and delicate humor redeems the volume's perversions of language both to make human communication possible and to incorporate the bestial into a context of love.

In its forming around two possible time perspectives, the structure of the poem also reflects the new possibility of relief. First is the cycle of nature evoked by the passage from winter to spring, by Lowell's changed age, and by the identification he feels with the flower who could not "meet another year's snowballing ennervation." Like the flower, he is now almost a weed, "frizzled, stale, and small." But there is another time. Lowell can be told "nothing's gone" because the family in some ways transcends time. Thirteen weeks absence have not changed his daughter. She "still" plays the same game and wants the same family ritual. This second time (similar to and yet so different from the ossification in McLean's) makes possible a human or symbolic view of the time lost at McLean's. For in traditional human terms the progress from winter to spring is never just a duration; it is also part of a rebirth cycle. Cured now, the frizzled Lowell can at least hope for the new future despaired of in the preceding poem.

The final sub-section of the volume both recapitulates the horrors of a purely naturalistic world (especially in the figure of Lepke and the animal images of " 'To Speak of Woe That Is in Marriage' ") and continues the possibility for secular redemption (in the baptism of his wife's loving "tirade" which in "Man and Wife" serves to alleviate the violence running through the volume by incorporating it into the context of family love). The ultimate confidence that secular redemption is really possible, however, comes only with what Lowell called the "affirmation" in "Skunk Hour" (O, 107). This affirmation is realized in two ways. First, the poem most directly faces the horror of the void created by the absence of values ("nobody's here"). Only in a dark night of the soul (a dark night Lowell calls "secular, puritan, and agnostical," O, 107) can true redemption be discovered. This is the importance of the Satan allusion: hell must be seen before one can mount the secular winding backstairs on top of which Lowell stands at the poem's conclusion. Second, Lowell tells us, "Skunk Hour is not entirely independent, but the anchor poem in its sequence" (O, 108). As such, it returns to and transforms almost all of the motifs which throughout the volume had suggested the horrors of the prose world. "Beyond the Alps" began *Life Studies* with a journey in spring, a kind of "Wasteland" spring with its stress on the difficulties involved in being reborn. "Skunk Hour" offers another journey, this time in the fall—the time for harvesting what was planted in the spring. At the same time, the fall setting allows the poem to begin with a restatement of the emptiness and desolation which have permeated the volume. And, as Hugh Staples points out, the first four stanzas present complementing images of a failing New England tradition.[10]

The desolation of the opening scenes leads to the poem's dramatic core where the essential struggle is to find some substance, some vital principle Lowell can reach out for to affirm his existence. John Berryman has shown how even the careful details of the initial stanzas are a defense against being swept away into the void of an attack of madness and this sense of emptiness is intensified by the parody of love Lowell gazes on. Surrounded by almost medieval reminders of human inadequacy (the cemetery and reference to the hill's "skull"), the lovers have no real human existence. As he also does in the

---

[10] Staples, p. 83.

brilliant opening lines of "Concord," Lowell suggests that the people are completely lost in their objects: "love-cars. . .lay together, hull to hull" and play songs whose words are banal and yet are ironically juxtaposed to the scene. The combination of emptiness and attempts at love throws Lowell back into his own loneliness, his own fear that he lacks any sense of inner principle ("I myself am hell;/nobody's here—"). Now, however, the animal images, which had served to reinforce the degradation felt when one is left with only a prose world, return to relieve the despair. For Lowell finds something in the skunk—a determination and a vitality that affirm at least life, and perhaps even a sense of responsibility, as values. Lowell in fact uses the word "soles" to suggest that through the bestial more than the bestial is found. The skunk accepts its responsibilities for its family and takes an active role in meeting dangers that threaten the fulfillment of these responsibilities. The rediscovery of the human through the bestial is also evoked by the skunk's final swilling from the garbage pail. Berryman suggests that this last action is a parody of the Eucharist and concludes a series of Christian over-tones in the poem.[11] The full significance of these overtones, of course, is that they redeem the empty rituals, especially eating and communion rituals, which have run through the volume, and suggest some success in Lowell's quest to replace religious with secular values. They also provide a parodic coup de grace to the garbage cans that Commander Lowell lettered, thinking church beneath the dignity of a naval man.

The end of the poem provides a perfect emblem of secular communion. Through the skunk as it makes its way under the "chalk-dry church spire" which provides an ironic reminder of the dead vertical world Lowell realizes values which enable him to conquer his despair. In fact, the context of the volume allows the skunk to play a redeeming role analogous to the one played by Christ in *Lord Weary's Castle*. And this communion has metapoetic impli-cations. Not only does the suggestion in "Words for Hart Crane" that art can become a mode of sympathizing with others reach a kind of fulfillment in the poem, but the emblem of the skunk suggests a new secular mode for art. As it swills the garbage in its desperate quest to live and provide for its family, it is doing exactly what Lowell does with his past in *Life Studies*. And, the volume successfully completed, Lowell too "will not scare." At the end of his essay on "Skunk Hour," Lowell returns to one of the basic motifs in the volume to summarize the importance of this last poem, "With Berryman, too, I go on a strange journey! Thank God, we both come out clinging to spars, enough floating matter to save us, though faith-less" (O, 110).

[11] For Berryman's comments cited in my discussion see Ostroff, pp. 99-100, 103-104. For a good example of Lowell's tendency to conceive religious ritual in secular terms, see his brilliant discussion of Lincoln's Gettysburg Address. He calls the address "a symbolic and sacramental act" and goes on to discuss the speech as the culmination of "a Christian sacrificial act of death and rebirth" (AT, 41).

A. Alvarez

Robert Lowell in Conversation

I

Robert Lowell, who was in London briefly for last week's Poetry Festival, is a tall, stooping man of great sensitivity, tact and an almost saint-like gentleness; he is also the foremost poet to emerge from America since the days of Eliot, Pound and Stevens. He is one of the Boston Lowells—who "talk to the Cabots"—and like Eliot he is a Harvard man, though he didn't stick it out, finishing at Kenyon College under the poet John Crowe Ransom.

He published his first two books, *Land of Unlikeness* and *Lord Weary's Castle,* in 1944 and 1946, when he himself was in his middle twenties. They caused an explosion in the literary world. Not only did they earn him all the usual prizes—and some unusual ones, including a Pulitzer—but they also clearly signalled the arrival of a totally new and independent talent, who had learned and assimilated the lessons of the great moderns, and applied them in ways wholly his own.

Thirteen years later, in 1959, came *Life Studies,* a complete and unexpected change in direction. In it he turned away from the more formal subjects and methods, and from the Catholic symbolism of his earlier work, and wrote rather loose, highly varied poems of an intimately autobiographical kind. It was another breakthrough in verse and has been much imitated.

Last year his volume of very free translations, *Imitations,* showed his style changing yet again. The poems since then have left *Life Studies* a long way behind. Now, at 46, he is at the height of his powers, the mature master of his own poetic world and style.

ALVAREZ: *People are continually claiming to find new directions in poetry—in your own included. How do you feel about it?*

LOWELL: Literary life is just one little wave after another: there was the Auden wave and the Dylan Thomas and the anti-Dylan Thomas, and we've had similar things in America. Most of the good poetry does seem to come out of these waves, though you occasionally get solitary figures who have nothing to do with them. The waves usually recede. There are few survivors: most people are left stranded on the beach.

One manner seems as bad or as good as another; it freshens the atmosphere

Part I from The London *Observer*, July 21, 1963, p. 19. Part II from *Review*, No. 8 (August 1963), pp. 36-40. Reprinted by permission of Robert Lantz-Candida Donadio Literary Agency, Inc.

for a moment and then seems to have faults as disastrous as the ones they were fighting against. Every so often something enormous opens, such as French symbolism, which will go on for 50 or 60 years with enormous talents one after another taking it up and changing it.

—Yet you yourself have certainly added something quite new to modern poetry. As I read it, it's a matter of coping with material which has not really been coped with before—taboo material, about a nervous breakdown and so on. There had been poems about these things before, but they were all in regular metre. What you've done is to let the metrical form shape itself out of the feelings.

LOWELL: Well, I remember I started one of these poems in Marvell's four-foot couplet and showed it to my wife. And she said "Why not say what really happened?" (It wasn't the one about her.) The metre just seemed to prevent any honesty on the subject, it got into the cadence of the four-foot couplet. The style came out of a whole lot of things, and I don't know myself what was the dominating influence.

In the beginning you got people who said this was prose and so forth and didn't want to see the skill, I think. Now you're beginning to get a time when there's too much of this confessional verse—in my own country it's one of the trends—and you feel that a lot of the poems don't have enough lyrical concentration.

I think a confessional poem is a possibility but you shouldn't overwork it. Often you have nothing to confess that makes a poem. The problem is to use a little of all that and be inventive. I think of several possibilities, of strings one might be able to pull: one is the confession given rather directly with hidden artifice; the other is a more rhetorical poem that doesn't use natural language at all; and then there are ways of distorting the experience, bringing in invention.

—The inspiration of this has nothing to do with "True Confessions." It's in recognizing what makes you tick, isn't it?

LOWELL: Well, the needle that prods into what really happened may be the same needle that writes a good line, I think. There's some sort of technical connection; there must be at best. Inspiration's such a tricky word, but we all know poetry isn't a craft that you can just turn on and off. It has to strike fire somewhere, and truth, maybe unpleasant truth about yourself, may be the thing that does that.

It's puzzling. You may be in a very sunny mood and the poem that comes out is not at all sunny; and to a certain extent vice versa. You can say that what comes out is your real self in some queer way, but it may be one that you're not particularly aware of at the time. Certainly, you can't trust your feelings and put them down and say "That's the truth." You find that often you're working with something that isn't your immediate feeling at all. I think it must be worked up.

When I was writing my book I had a lot of argument with action painters. I wanted to return to a sort of Tolstoyan fullness of representation, and their technical freedom came from doing the opposite. Yet I suppose there's some connection. Something pushed the two of us at the same time, it seems to me: action painting and my kind of writing. Mine seemed to bring in more and more human experience. Theirs left it out entirely. I feel it's a narrow kind of painting and that it reaches a limit, whereas the kind of thing I do, if someone of greater power did it, is limitless, it seems to me.

—Obviously, this kind of writing involves a great deal of strain. Was it to alleviate that that you turned to plays?

LOWELL: Yes, and on a small scale—I mean, I don't know too much about writing plays. I found it a great relief to have a plot and people who weren't me at all. I could say things that were personal that I couldn't say in a confessional poem. I don't mean that I know how to write a play as well as a poem, but the medium gave a certain freedom.

—Is this why you do translations as well?

LOWELL: I think so. The centre's provided, the plot of the poem, even the tone, and then you're free to let yourself go at that point. When I was doing Villon and Rimbaud and Baudelaire I tried to live through the plots of their poems. It was as if I'd been given Villon's costume for a little while. It's a great soothing.

—Do you think that the seriousness of your verse—your willingness and ability to tackle difficult new subjects—is linked with the professionalism of American literary life? We, by contrast, seem so debilitatingly amateur.

LOWELL: I think it's the sort of "all-outness" which the Americans perhaps have that's a virtue. But the trouble with our professionalism is that it becomes a little bit too much an abstract technique which really, I think, isn't technique in some sense. There's too much concentration on how a poem's made. And actually someone who seems rather imperfect such as Wordsworth, who can write bad lines and good lines, is a master technician in the kind of resources he can use and put into poetry.

From my point of view Philip Larkin is the English poet I follow most carefully. He seems utterly professional and a technician in a way almost no American is. As for Ted Hughes, I find him just a sort of thunderbolt. His animal poems are some of the best poems in English. I wouldn't know whether he could influence anybody; whether he's typical of any country.

—*What about Auden and Dylan Thomas? Do you feel any links with them?*

LOWELL: Well, when I first read Thomas in the Faber book about 1935 he appealed to me very much in that he was metrical and splendid and non-political in any direct sense. But I think it's a poetry that's limited. He's certainly a great poet in about 10 poems, the sheer energy of it. But I find him less interesting than Auden. Auden has made that period immortal, that period of waiting for the war.

My first book was written *during* the war, which was a very different time from the thirties. Then violence, heroism, things like that, seemed much more natural to life. They seemed everyday matters and that governed my style. Things seemed desperate. Even though our cities weren't bombed you felt they might be, and we were destroying thousands of people. The world seemed apocalyptic at that time, and heroically so. I thought that civilisation was going to break down, and instead *I* did.

—*What connection do you think there is between your present verse and your political situation—or your country's?*

LOWELL: I'm very conscious of belonging to the country I do, which is a very powerful country and, if I have an image of it, it would be one taken from Melville's *Moby Dick:* the fanatical idealist who brings the world down in ruins through some sort of simplicity of mind. I believe that's in our character and in my own personal character; I reflect that it's a danger for us. It's not all on the negative side, but there's power there and energy and freshness and the possibility of ruin. I'm very aware of that.

I lost sleep about the atom bomb, of course. I don't think this is a period of parties and politics, the way the thirties were. Here and in America that all seems to have calmed down to something we imagine is more the way life ordinarily is. While in the thirties everybody was taking sides on something, usually very violently. The whole thing was almost like snakes twisting and hissing at each other. Things couldn't be more different now, in fact people are rather nostalgic for it.

—*Well, how do you see the situation now?*

LOWELL: I think the thing Pasternak expressed is universal . . . and it's certainly very strong in my country: that is, the danger of the great impersonal bureaucratic machine rolling over everything and flattening out humanity; the danger of luxury and organisation and all this slick stuff, this vulgarity and so forth. That's the terrible danger.

II

ALVAREZ: *Your verse has changed a great deal, hasn't it? Most of the mannerisms of rhythm and imagery that you used in your early poems have disappeared, and yet you now have something much more personal. Is this how you see your own work?*

LOWELL: When my second book came out the most interesting review of it was by Randall Jarrell. Though he liked the book, he made the point that I was doing things I could do best quite often, and I think he quoted Kipling— when you learn how to do something, don't do it again. I think you should always do something a little longer than you should, go on until it gives out. There was a long pause between the second and the third. I didn't want to go just cranking the same machine.

—When your first poems came out you were a Catholic, weren't you? You've ceased to be one since. Has the change in style anything to do with this change in allegiance?

LOWELL: It may have. In the second book I wasn't a Catholic but I was using Catholic material from a non-Catholic point of view, a neutral one. In *Life Studies* I was very anxious to get a tone that sounded a little like conversation.

—I felt that in Life Studies *you were setting your personal house in order, you were dealing with very personal material almost as you would in psychoanalysis. It seemed that, having left behind the dogmatic Catholic base and the dogmatic rhythms and symbols that went with it, you were trying to build a new base from which you could work.*

LOWELL: I had in the back of my mind something like the prose of a Chekhov short story. The poems came in two spurts. The first was more intense when two-thirds of the autobiographical poems were written. This was a period of, at most, three months. Then there was a second period which finished that group and filled in blank spaces.

—I remember someone in The Review *saying that the prose section in your book—which unfortunately wasn't published in the English version—was often more concentrated than one or two of the poems about your relatives. Do you think that's a fair comment?*

LOWELL: There's a long first section in *Life Studies* called "Last Afternoon with Uncle Devereux Winslow" which was originally written in prose. I put it aside and I later cut things out and re-arranged it and made different transitions and put it into verse, so there is that connection and perhaps the style comes out of writing prose. But I'd say that the prose was an awful job to do. It took a long time and I think it could be less concentrated with more sting or something like that.

—You don't find prose comes naturally?

LOWELL: I find it very hard. I like to revise and when you have something of thirty or forty pages written as carefully as a poem— and it was written that carefully—it's very hard.

—Do you revise your poems much?

LOWELL: Usually. I think my record is a poem that was finished in one day. Usually it's a long time. I would have said that writing free verse you're more likely to get a few lines that are right in the beginning than you are in metre.

—My own interpretation of Life Studies *is that the family poems cleared the ground and that, with the now very famous poems like "Man and Wife," "Home After Three Months Away," and "Waking in the Blue," your own voice came up absolutely clear—they have this unmistakable Lowell rhythm.*

LOWELL: They are not written chronologically. Actually the first poem finished was "Skunk Hour" and I think the second was "Man and Wife," though they were all going on at the same time. But the first nut to crack really was "Skunk Hour"—that was the hardest. I cast about . . . it was written backwards, more or less, and I added the first four stanzas after I'd finished it.

—It came before these family poems?

LOWELL: Yes, actually it was the first, although the others were sort of started. I guess the first thing I had was a very imperfect version of "Man and Wife," which I dropped, and then I wrote "Skunk Hour." "Skunk Hour" was the first one completed. I was reading Elizabeth Bishop's poems very carefully at the time and imitating the loose formality of her style.

—It seems to me that that poem is less successful in its opening lines. It suddenly gets down to what you're really talking about in the last part.

LOWELL: The opening's sort of cotton-nosed, it's supposed to let you sink into the poem and then it tenses up. I don't know whether it works or not. You dawdle in the first part and suddenly get caught in the poem.

—Confessional verse as you write it isn't simply an outpouring, is it? It's very strict, although the rules are hard to find.

LOWELL: You're asking how a confessional poem that's a work of art differs from someone's outpourings, sensational confessions for the newspapers or confessions to one's analyst. It seems to me there is some connection. When I was doing what might be called confessional poems there was a big chunk of something to be gotten out, but a great deal of it was very tame; the whole thing wasn't any very great story, but still there were things I wanted to say. Then the thing was the joy of composition, to get some music and imagination and form into it and to know just when to stop and what sort of language to put in it—it was pure joy writing it and I think it was pure technical joy, and poems are dull if you don't have that.

—What about the technique? You were saying that you have a great love for William Carlos Williams, who I would say seems to be the antithetical poet to you. Has he had any effect?

LOWELL: I always liked Williams, since I was a young man. But I don't think I've ever written anything that's very much like him. He really is utterly carried away into the object, it intoxicated him in describing it, and his way of composition's so different from mine. He was an active doctor and he wrote in snatches; he developed a way of writing in which he could get things out very quickly. I find him a very artful poet, but his art was largely cutting what he poured out. My things are much more formal, much more connected with older English poetry; there's a sort of formal personality in myself. I think anyone could tell that my free verse was written by someone who'd done a lot of formal verse. I began writing in the thirties and the current I fell into was the southern group of poets—John Crowe Ransom and Allen Tate— and that was partly a continuation of Pound and Eliot and partly an attempt to make poetry much more formal than Eliot and Pound did: to write in metres but to make the metres look hard and make them hard to write. It was the period of the famous book *Understanding Poetry*, of analysing poems to see how they're put together; there was a great emphasis on craftsmanship. Out of that, though it came later, were poetry workshops and all that sort of thing. Well, that's in my blood very much, and about 1950 it was prevailing everywhere in America. There were poets trained that way, writing in the style, writing rather complicated, difficult, laboured poems, and it was getting very dry. You felt you had to get away from that at all costs. Yet still it's in one's blood. We're trained that way and I admire Tate and Ransom as much as ever. But in England that was the period of Auden and poetry was trying to express the times, politics, psychology, economics, the war and everything that somehow wasn't very strong with us. We had such poets and we had a lot of Auden imitators, but the strongest feeling seemed to be to get away from that and just write a poem. We talked a lot about form, craft, tragic experience and things like that.

—On this question of Auden, you seem to feel apparently quite strongly about not being political.

LOWELL: Well, yes, and that's quite misleading because it now seems to me that Auden's glory is that he caught all those things with much greater power than any of the people of his group. He's made the period immortal, of waiting for the war. At that time it seemed so stifled in controversy that it wasn't possible for us. People tried it in our country.

—What he got really was not the politics but the neurotic tension.

LOWELL: That's a better description. He caught the air and it was air in which events were hovering over your shoulder at every point, the second war was boiling into existence. Freud and Marx and a host of thinkers who were the most alive at that time—and still are in many ways—all do get into his poetry, and the idiom of those people waiting! I find that marvellous. I don't think this is a period of parties and politics the way the thirties were. Here and in America that all seems to have calmed down to something we imagine is more the way life ordinarily is. I don't meet people who are violently anti-Russian very often. That doesn't seem to be the air.

—They still exist, though.

LOWELL: They exist, but they don't exist very much in the intellectual world. While in the thirties everybody was taking sides on something, usually very violently—violent conversions, violent Marxist positions, violent new deal, violent anti-new deal—things couldn't be more different now. The terrible danger now is of the great impersonal bureaucratic machinery rolling over everything and flattening out humanity.

—The poets over here, and I would say in the States too, with the Beats, are rather cashing in on this.

LOWELL: Well, some of the Beats are quite good, but no mass movement like that can be of much artistic importance. It was a way for people to get away from the complexities of life. You've got to remain complicatedly civilised and organised to keep your humanity under the pressures of our various governments, not go into a bohemian wildness. Quite a few people are genuinely bohemian; the real bohemia is something tremendous, of course. I think someone really good, some Hart Crane, might swoop down on all this material and take it up and make art out of it. It's useful in a way that a certain amount of ice has been broken.

—Do you believe in poets ganging together in schools and groups and movements and so on?

LOWELL: Literary life is just one little wave after another: there was the Auden wave and the Dylan Thomas and the anti-Dylan Thomas, and we've had similar things. Most of the good poetry does seem to come out of these waves, though you occasionally get solitary figures who have nothing to do with them. But there are few survivors, most people are left stranded on the beach. One manner seems as bad or as good as another; it freshens the atmosphere for a moment and then seems to have faults equally as disastrous as the ones it was fighting against. But what's important, every so often something enormous opens, such as French symbolism, which will go on for fifty or sixty years, with enormous talents one after another taking it up and changing it. To a certain extent we have this in America in the generation of Pound and Eliot and Marianne Moore.

[Published by permission of "The Observer" who commissioned the interview from which these extracts are selected. Further extracts can be found in "The Observer" of July 21, 1963. Ed.]

A. Alvarez

A Talk with Robert Lowell

This conversation took place in the studio where Robert Lowell works, a couple of floors above his family apartment. It's a high, very private room in a pleasantly old-fashioned block just off Central Park West. The view is undramatic yet specifically New York: the oddly shapeless backs of big buildings, water-towers, airshafts, and those deep narrow wells called "backyards." Unlike most New York flats, this one is peculiarly silent. The perpetual honking of car horns never penetrates this far back. Only occasionally the central heating creaks and bangs mildly. Otherwise there is nothing to distract you.

Lowell himself, now in his middle forties, is a big man, yet rather frail. His manner is gentle, almost saintly, although he can, when appropriate, be tart enough in his comments, a mixture of shyness and stringency, relaxed yet with a great deal in reserve. He is now at the height of his creative powers as a poet. He began his career as something of a prodigy, with two brilliant and influential books published in his middle twenties: *Land of Unlikeness* and

From *Encounter,* XXIV (February 1965), 39-43. Reprinted by permission of Robert Lantz-Candida Donadio Literary Agency, Inc.

Lord Weary's Castle. Like Dylan Thomas, he seemed to have given a new edge to poetic language, post-Eliot, symbolic, Catholic, and with powerfully original rhythms. Then there was a long pause, until thirteen years later he produced *Life Studies*—totally new, moving in a totally different direction, and even more influential. The Catholicism and symbolism had gone; the texture was simpler and the effort was to deal with his experience as nakedly as possible, letting the flow of feeling regulate the rhythmical pattern, which remained as insistently individual as ever. That was in 1959. In 1962 he published an extraordinary book of free translations called *Imitations*, really original variations by Lowell on themes from other poets. He has also translated Racine's *Phèdre* and recently completed a play of his own, *The Old Glory,* based on short stories by Nathaniel Hawthorne and Herman Melville, which Jonathan Miller has just directed in New York with success. In *Imitations* and in the collection of new poems which he has made since then and which has just been published in the States, Lowell seems to have reached a new stage of technical and emotional fluency. In his early poems the power was sometimes short-circuited by mannerisms: the language could be too clotted, the rhythms almost predictably idiosyncratic. In *Life Studies* these mannerisms were reversed: some of the weaker poems were so loose, almost prattling, that the poetic urgency seemed to drain away in personal reminiscence. (I had better admit that this is critical hindsight. Each book of Lowell's seems, to an extraordinary degree, complete and resolved in itself. Then the next one appears and goes so unexpectedly far beyond the last that you have to revise your demands. He has, in short, a genius for constantly setting and then raising the standards by which his own work is to be judged.) But since *Imitations* the barriers have been down between his technique and his emotional resources, his imaginative power effortlessly matching the depth and scope and continual richness of his responses. His work now has that rare aliveness and vibration that comes only in the maturity of a major artist.

When we talked he had recently been ill and his reactions had the slightly tentative directness and openness, that curiously new-born quality, which goes with convalescence. And this tone seemed to match very precisely the raw, nervous atmosphere of New York in the period following President Kennedy's assassination, with its odd feeling of general psychic shock and displacement.

I began by asking him why the American artists, who are usually not in the least concerned with politicians, seemed to identify so closely with the dead President.

LOWELL:, Well, Kennedy represents a side of America that is appealing to the artist in retrospect, a certain heroism. You feel in certain terms he really was a martyr in his death; that he was reckless, went further than the office called for, and perhaps that he was fated to be killed. That's an image one could treasure, and it stirs one.

—But it's not just an image that concerns you. Don't you identify more with Kennedy than with other Presidents, because he somehow changed the position of the artist in American society, raised his status, and made him more acceptable by his obvious and publicly manifested interest in the cultural life of the country? I mean he invited artists and intellectuals to the Inauguration and to those White House dinner parties, he gave them medals and awards, he brought August Heckscher to the White House as his Special Consultant on the Arts, and so on.

LOWELL: I think you can take two more or less opposed lines on Kennedy: that the arts were in some way getting, though they haven't become more popular, more and more prestige, so that finally (as Hannah Arendt says) it wasn't so much that Kennedy wanted to do anything for the arts but just his own personal ambition wanted to include the arts, and have the artists come to the White House. . . . But it was part of his ambition to tap this latent prestige of the arts. Well, the other line is that he was really a very exceptional President who broke the ice and put the artists sort of in the front window for a moment.

—Yet those dinner parties of Kennedy's did have some curious side-effects, didn't they? Weren't they, if nothing else, a sign of change? I mean when Eisenhower was President you felt that the country was being run exclusively by the Pentagon and those awful golfing big-business cronies of his. With Kennedy there did seem some vague, fragile possibility of some kind of connection, even mutual interchange, between the representatives of the cultural life of the country and those of the world of power.

LOWELL: I think of Edmund Wilson's comment. Arthur Schlesinger asked him how he felt about being invited to the White House to dinner and Wilson said "Oh, it was bigger than other dinners! . . ." I was invited to the White House for Malraux's dinner there. Kennedy made a rather graceful joke that "the White House was becoming almost a café for intellectuals. . . ." Then we all drank a great deal at the White House, and had to sort of be told not to take our champagne into the concert, and to put our cigarettes out like children—though nicely, it wasn't peremptory. Then the next morning you read that the Seventh Fleet had been sent somewhere in Asia and you had a funny feeling of how unimportant the artist really was: that this was sort of window dressing and that the real government was somewhere else, and that something much closer to the Pentagon was really ruling the country. And maybe this is how it must be.

You see, I have a feeling that the arts are in a very funny position now—that we are free to say what we want to, and somehow what we want to say is the confusion and sadness and incoherence of the human condition. Anyone running a government must say the opposite of that: that it can be solved. He must take an optimistic stance. I don't know why the arts say this so strongly. It may be a more miserable time, more than others, with the world liable to blow up. We're in some transition domestically: I mean in one's family life and everything else. There are new moral possibilities, new moral incoherence. It's a very confused moment. And for some reason it's almost a dogma with us: we'll show that confusion.

—The confusion has been staring right at you since the events in Dallas, hasn't it? But I wonder if the pervasiveness and inescapability of it all isn't emphasized by the American preoccupation with psycho-analysis. Everybody is in analysis. It's the dominant mode for the American interpretation of reality. And whatever you think about it, it does at least force one to recognise the answering confusion in oneself. Analysis has made it very difficult to live purely *rationally and on the surface, at least with any conviction.*

LOWELL: Well, I get a funny thing from psycho-analysis. I mean Freud is the man who moves me most: and his case histories, and the book on dreams, read almost like a late Russian novel to me—with a scientific rather than a novelist's mind. They have a sort of marvellous old-order quality to them, though he is the father of the new order, almost the opposite of what psycho-analysis has been since. All that human sort of colour and sadness, that long German-Austrian and Jewish culture that Freud had, seems something in the past; but it was still real to him. There is something rather beautiful and sad and intricate about Freud that seems to have gone out of psycho-analysis; it's become a way of looking at things.

—What I suppose you're getting at is a certain moral rooted quality in Freud—a sense of continuing cultural tradition which you don't get in the orthodox Freudians.

LOWELL: I was brought up as an Episcopalian Protestant, with a good deal of Bible reading at school. We had a rather sceptical attitude, but we were rather saturated (even in this late day) with it. And it strikes me this may be just true of my own peculiar history: brought up as a Protestant, then a Catholic convert. When that goes and we look at it another way, Freud seems the only religious teacher. I have by no means a technical understanding of Freud, but he's very much part of my life. He seems unique among the non-fictional teachers of the century. He's a prophet. I think somehow he continues both the Jewish and Christian tradition, and puts it maybe in a much more rational position. I find nothing bores me more than someone who has all the orthodox sort of Freudian answers like the Catechism, but what I find about Freud is that he provides the conditions that one must think in. I'm thinking of my own case: I'm one-eighth Jewish and seven-eighths non-Jewish and our culture seems sort of that way. We never supplied what the Jewish tradition did—our culture never supplied the equivalent of that. And now to-day, we can't. The two thinkers, non-fictional thinkers, who influence and are never out of one's mind are Marx and Freud.

—Now this, of course, is particularly so in New York, which is enormously Jewish in its whole atmosphere, isn't it? The intellectual life is almost entirely Jewish, most of the entertaining is Jewish, the ways of eating are Jewish, and so on.

LOWELL: Yes, and I think there wouldn't be any active American culture now without the Jewish element. They are small in numbers, but they're a leaven that changes the whole intellectual, cultural world of America. And it's a painful reality, I think, that a minority should have such liveliness and vigour that you're at a loss why the rest of the country doesn't equal that.

—There is every reason why the Jews should feel at home in the States. I mean American democracy was based, theoretically, on certain abstract principles which were lacking in Europe. So the Jews, as more or less permanent outsiders in Europe, would have responded to America very strongly.

LOWELL: I think of Jefferson and the whole idealism—there are very few countries founded on a declaration the way ours was. There's something biblical and Jewish about that—Messianic. It is both what is unreal about America and what's noble about America. Violence and idealism have some occult connection. I remember reading Henry Adams' *History of Jefferson and Madison*—it's rather sceptical history, far from idealising America (though it's different from Adams' later position). I noticed the strange pride that Adams takes in American gunnery—it's almost wild-Western: that the American ships shot better than the English ships and that Andrew Jackson's artillery shot better than the British artillery. All that had some great symbolic significance to him. We seem to be a very sheer country: I mean power is something everyone must have, because the country's powerful. The ideal isn't real unless it's somehow backed by power. Robert Frost was very much criticised for his remark about poetry and power: "We must have more of both." Well, he seemed to rejoice in that. But in a way I feel it is our curse that we can't disentangle those two things.

—Well, power and violence—above all, violence—are things you simply can't get away from in the States: they seem to come in at you from every direction.

LOWELL: I don't know where it comes from—whether it's the American genius, or just the chaos of our schools and that young people are badly brought up—but I think it has something to do with both the idealism and the power of the country. Other things are boring for these young people, and violence isn't boring. We have a thing for the Western movie: some sort of faith that the man who can draw most quickly is the real hero. He's proved himself. Yet that is a terribly artificial standard; the real hero might be someone who'd never get his pistol out of the holster, stumbling about, near-sighted. We don't want to admit that. It's deep in us that the man who draws first somehow has proved himself.

—But this violence and heroism is in key with the tone of the country: with the speed, the rawness, the vast size, the emptiness and the aggression of the cities.

LOWELL: I feel that it's a very naked country; the sort of flesh that goes on the skeleton and the nervous system that works is very meagre. And we come to Norman Mailer—he has this peculiar thing, he's cursed with it. The country works so well; it's powerful; therefore the writers should be on an enormous scale. And why can't we produce an enormous novel, the way the Russians did in the nineteenth century? It's quite beyond our powers, apparently, though maybe some American will appear who'll disprove that. But there's a burden on Mailer to make that attempt, and we're cursed with the ambitious big novel. Yet it's not entirely a curse and Mailer is genuinely a hero and every so often he really does have the flesh so that he's at least the greatest of our journalists, I think; suddenly all those enormous ambitions get clothed for a moment.

—So you think that this ambition and power—the kind of thing you get in Mailer—is specifically an American characteristic?

LOWELL: We have some impatience with prosaic, everyday things of life— I think those hurt us. That sort of whimsical patience that other countries may have—that's really painful to endure: to be minor. We leap for the sublime. You might almost say American literature and culture begins with *Paradise Lost.* I always think there are two great symbolic figures that stand behind American ambition and culture. One is Milton's Lucifer and the other is Captain Ahab: these two sublime ambitions that are doomed and ready, for their idealism, to face any amount of violence.

—Does this literary, spiritual quality also affect America's political behaviour?

LOWELL: Our world position is a curious sort of fulfilment of a national characteristic: that we're a country founded on a constitution. That makes us rather different from the usual country founded on a history and a culture. We were founded on a Declaration, on the Constitution, on Principles, and we've always had the ideal of "saving the world." And that comes close to perhaps destroying the world. Suddenly it is as though this really terrible nightmare has come true, that we are suddenly in a position where we might destroy the world, and that is very closely allied to saving it. We might blow up Cuba to save ourselves and then the whole world would blow up. Yet it would come in the guise of an idealistic stroke.

—But the trouble with this idealism is that it seems so unqualified at times: I mean the anti-Communism, you know. The anti-totalitarianism is so overwhelming that it becomes at times something very like another form of totalitarianism, certainly, a kind of total stupidity.

LOWELL: Yes, I suppose this is too apocalyptic to put it this way, but it is the Ahab story of having to murder evil: and you may murder all the good with it if it gets desperate enough to struggle. Russia is in somewhat the same position, of course. It is a world situation now. But it hits our genius in a very strange way, and what's best in our country in a way is united with this, and what's worst and most dangerous and naked and inhuman about us gets swept up into this ideal. And also this thing that we won't let go, a kind of energy and power of imagination, of throwing yourself all out into something.

—And does this affect the arts—the idea of never having minor art, the one thing no one can bear to be is minor?

LOWELL: Yes. It's often said that we have no minor poets in America, though of course we do; but that seems an oddly ignoble ambition. Even the minor poet reaches for the sublime.

—What about the theory that sociology is taking over the arts? Isn't there a perfectly good case to be made for the first great American novel being not Moby Dick *or* The Scarlet Letter *but de Tocqueville's* Democracy in America?

LOWELL: But would you call de Tocqueville a sociologist? His book still seems the best book on America, and it's an oddly unique book. He somehow lived it, yet it's a rather abstract book. Still, it's a book he couldn't have written without having visited America and lived through it; that's always there.

—But this abstractness is somehow typical: for example, the big political issues which are plaguing you now—"Civil rights" and "poverty"—are essentially moral, slightly abstract issues, not party issues. I mean that, except for the extremists on the right, both parties agree that these are national sick-

*nesses that must be cured. They merely disagree about the kind and the
quantity of medicine needed.*

LOWELL: This may not answer what you're after at all. The biggest issue
in the country now is civil rights. We're bound to act morally on this and, of
course, there's the danger that the morals may cut people's legs off; they may
be simplified. The only opposition to civil rights is an inarticulate immoral
position that has a certain human appeal, I think—the Southern. But it's
morally indefensible. This seems to come down all the way from the Civil
War, that the Southerner's morally inarticulate. One felt this more strongly in
the 'thirties when there was a "Southern Renaissance" in culture. It was,
perhaps, the strongest single element in American culture: this Southern position which somehow was quite human and observant (in some ways typically
American, but in others not), and it was a sort of position with its moral head
cut off. Somehow this whole Southern view didn't make sense morally; but it
was observant of life and talked a great deal about the "tragedy of life." The
Southerners no longer seem to have that strength. When you have a rather
disagreeable reactionary Southerner talking, it is terrible that he doesn't make
more sense, moral sense.

*—Does this lack of "moral sense" have something to do with the general
rootlessness and mobility of American life? It is something that strikes the
visitor very hard: nothing seems to last, neither objects, nor relationships, nor
even the landscape. And people are always drifting restlessly from one city to
another, eternally migrating.*

LOWELL: The mobility I know most about in America is New York City.
And this is such a cliché I blush to utter it. But you go from New York to
London—and they're two cities in many ways much alike, maybe essentially
alike—but the superficial difference hits you terribly hard. You can't touch a
stone in London that doesn't point backwards into history; while even for an
American city, New York seems to have no past. And yet it's the only city
that sort of provides an intellectual, human continuum to live in. Of course
you don't have to live in New York. Many people loathe living in it. But still,
if you removed it, you'd be cutting out the heart of American culture. Yet it
is a heart with no past. The New York of fifty years ago is utterly gone and
there are no landmarks; the record of the city doesn't point back into the
past. It has that sheer presence which, I think, is not the image of mobility
you talk about.

*—This kind of driving force, moving into the future all the time, without a
past at all, as though the wake were closing up behind it. . . .*

LOWELL: And it has a great sheer feeling of utter freedom. And then
when one thinks back a little bit, it seems all confused and naked.

—Do you think this freedom is behind the cult of experimentalism of America in the arts, the demand that no two poets, no two major poets in America ever write the same?

LOWELL: Well, certainly they are not burdened down with this sort of baggage of life the English poet carries. I mean what everyone finds wrong with American culture is the monotony of the sublime. I've never lived anywhere else, but I feel it is extreme (and perhaps unique, even) about America, that the artist's existence becomes his art. He is re-born in it, and he hardly exists without it. There's that feeling, perhaps.

—That he himself is as mobile as the society, he has no roots in the family, no real social niche, no sense of permanence?

LOWELL: A friend of mine went to London this summer. He was utterly delighted with it and said, "It's so human" (he comes from the South). "And its people were so polite, and it just seemed unimaginably gentle and wonderful in a way an American city isn't." But he avoided meeting any English literary people; he felt that England was a disaster for the literary man, that he was hampered at every step with "cautions and nots and things." That shows the American temperament, the impatience.

—Well, the major part of these "cautions and nots and things" is the compulsory Cult of the Amateur in England—which you certainly don't suffer from in the States.

LOWELL: We are talking about the arts being, perhaps, more a profession in the States. I don't know enough about Englishmen or any other country to make a comparison. But I feel this in meeting people, that we have a feeling the arts should be "all out"—you're in it, you're all out in it, and you're not ashamed to talk about it endlessly, sheerly. That would seem embarrassing to an Englishman, and inhuman, probably, to be that "all out" about it. I guess the American finds something a little uninvigorating about the Englishman that he doesn't do that.

—There is this terrible feeling in England that excellence is something that, in a sense, one ought to feel apologetic about.

LOWELL: Done with your left hand, and it's always done with both your hands in America. We were talking about it earlier: the artist finds new life in his art and almost sheds his other life.

G. S. Fraser

Amid the Horror, a Song of Praise

When Samson, in the Book of Judges, had killed a lion, he passed the same way some time later "and, behold, there was a swarm of bees and honey in the carcass of the lion." Offering the honey to his Philistine friends and in-laws, Samson asked them the riddle, "Out of the strong came forth sweetness," and they could not answer it. The story struck Yeats as a beautiful parable about the "unchristened heart" of the true poet who, like Homer, produces out of violence and rankness and death pure exultation. Of all living American and English poets, the parable applies best to Robert Lowell.

No other English or American poet of his generation has, in his handling of language, the same sheer brute strength; no other poet is so deeply moved not only by moral but by physical horror and disgust (which can include self-disgust), and by a kind of blind Samson-like ferocity. And yet, insensibly, in Lowell's hands the tale of the world's horrors becomes a tale of the world's wonders, the catalogue of obscure absurdities, a song of praise. And the lumbering, cumbrous, thick-thewed movement of his verse can ripple suddenly into a touchingly tender vulnerability, like Samson's vulnerability to Delilah.

Mr. Lowell's last volume of original poems, *Life Studies,* had a mixed reception. In England, A. Alvarez hailed it as a breakthrough to a new kind of poetry, one of raw, direct experience. But John Malcolm Brinnin told me that he thought *Life Studies* was a sad falling-off from the extreme intricate rhetorical formality, the elaborate religious symbolism, of Lowell's earlier poems. It seemed to him that, having created a beautiful public language, for the public theme of the Christian consciousness appalled by the hard heart of the modern world, Mr. Lowell had wantonly deserted this for excessively private psychoanalytical notebook jottings. *Life Studies* on the whole eschewed myth and legend, and found its main material in personal experience and family history. But it took a family history, like personal experience, as a set of brute particulars.

A fact, so to say, became "poetical" in its very irreducible factuality. Lowell's friends, his relations, his experiences in mental hospitals were in no sense generalized or clarified. Rather, they were named, in all their confusingness, as sacred objects in themselves. Similarly, Lowell's rhetoric in *Life Studies* became much looser and suppler than it had been in his earlier poems. The contrast was rather like that between the extreme formality of Ezra

From The *New York Times Book Review,* October 4, 1964, p. 1+. ©1964 by The New York Times Company. Reprinted by permission.

Pound's "Sestina: Altaforte" (1909) and the apparently off-the-cuff casualness of "Hugh Selwyn Mauberley" (1920). The earlier poems had been elaborately composed, "through-composed" in the musical sense, in difficult forms; the poems of *Life Studies* aimed at an appearance of improvisation and carelessly felicitous abruptness. If there was an esthetic moral to be drawn from *Life Studies,* it was that literally anything that happens to a poet, however chaotic, fragmentary, or absurd, can, without any sort of literary doctoring, suddenly become poetry.

This free-wheeling manner of composition obviously has its dangers. It could lead—and in some younger poets influenced by Mr. Lowell it does lead—to exhibitionism and raggedness. More subtly, it may lead to a kind of pumping up of emotions, a forcing of the note, a making more of a situation than is really in it. Yet Lowell's new volume, *For the Union Dead,* which seems to me the most powerful and direct volume of poems he has yet published, justifies those who like Alvarez (and like myself) welcomed his second manner. What can be seen now more clearly, however (and this may partly vindicate Brinnin), is that under the apparently casual surface of the second manner there lurks a power of concentrated phrasing and a gift of ordering, of subtle transitions of topic and mood to develop the full impact of a ruling theme, which has been earned by the more impersonal and more obviously formal discipline of the earlier poems.

Nor could *For the Union Dead,* like *Life Studies,* be accused of an excessive privacy. The imagination behind the poems is like the imagination of a great historian, reliving the past while relating it always to the troubles of the present; an imagination at once passionately literal and fiercely prophetic, like the imagination of Carlyle.

Let me try to illustrate both the historical range and that passionate exactness. In a poem on Buenos Aires, such a phrase as "the leaden, internecine generals," or such a stanza as this,

> Literal commemorative busts
> preserved the frogged coats
> [and fussy, furrowed foreheads
> of those soldier bureaucrats,

condenses miraculously what it would take a historian many pages or chapters to say about the sad, violent, and heavy farce of Argentine political history. Similarly, a poem on Jonathan Edwards seems to sum up all that one has read, or felt, by Edwards or about him. In his literalness, his fierceness, his occasional brutality, and in his deceptive casualness, Mr. Lowell seems extremely anti-academic. Yet in another sense he has a first-rate academic intellect, an instinctive feeling for the heart of a historical situation and an ability to relate it directly to a contemporary one.

The wonderful title poem, for instance, is partly a noble tribute to the heroism and idealism of the New England abolitionists; but it is partly also an indictment, fierce and vivid, of the decay of New England idealism, and of the indifference of Northern liberalism to what might be called the constructive meekness of Negroes in the United States today.

The central symbol of this poem is the statue, in Boston, of Colonel Shaw, who commanded a Negro battalion in the Civil War, and who stood for all the simple dignity and integrity of old Boston. Mr. Lowell counterpoints this image with one of modern Boston, shoddily destroying its own style and history:

> . . . One morning last March,
> I pressed against the new barbed and galvanized
>
> fence on the Boston Common. Behind their cage,
> yellow dinosaur steamshovels were grunting
> as they cropped up tons of mush and grass
> to gouge their underworld garage.

He counterpoints Colonel Shaw's image, also, with the image of our present callousness to violence and wrong:

> The ditch is nearer.
> There are no statues for the last war here;
> on Boylston Street, a commercial photograph
> shows Hiroshima boiling
>
> over a Mosler Safe, the "Rock of Ages"
> that survived the blast. Space is nearer.
> When I crouch to my television set,
> the drained faces of Negro school-children rise like balloons.

It is part of Mr. Lowell's strength in this volume that he is not merely a poetic consciousness, but a poetic conscience. By exposing himself so nakedly to the hurt of our times (and the hurt of his own raw awareness), he acquires the voice of a prophet, the right to denounce:

> . . . Everywhere,
> giant finned cars nose forward like fish;
> a savage servility
> slides by on grease.

The long fish-like cars suggest Shakespeare's "monsters of the deep," appetite preying on itself; the worst slavery is not the oppression of the Negroes but the blind appetitiveness of the indifferent whites, the obsequious conformists. Ironically, "servility"—the word is beautifully and exactly chosen here—is traditionally a vice of lackeys, not of smolderingly indignant slaves.

There are, of course, poems in this volume gentler and happier than this great title poem of prophetic denunciation. I think the mood is less consistently a painful one than the mood of *Life Studies*. There are even poems, like "Soft Wood," about the cleansing and purifying seascape of Maine, whose mood is predominantly one of affectionate gentleness:

> Here too in Maine things bend to the wind forever.
> After two years away, one must get used
> to the painted soft wood staying bright and clean,
> to the air blasting an all-white wall whiter,
> as it blows through curtain and screen
> touched with salt and evergreen.

There is, in another poem, a fine evocation of Hawthorne, for Mr. Lowell the one heroic figure among the Transcendentalists:

> The disturbed eyes rise,
> furtive, foiled, dissatisfied
> from meditation on the true
> and insignificant.

That might be a description also of Mr. Lowell's own baffled honesty and scrupulous exactness. But of course the true is never insignificant in the end.

Stanley Kunitz

Talk with Robert Lowell

Robert Lowell speaks with an air of gentle authority. Surprisingly, for a New Englander, his voice has a soft Southern tincture, which may be traced back to his formative years when he modeled himself on the Southerners Allen Tate and John Crowe Ransom. His wife, who supplies another auditory influence, is the Kentucky-born novelist and critic, Elizabeth Hardwick, one of the founding editors of The New York Review of Books.

Since 1960, when the Lowells braved the shock of transplanting themselves from Boston, they have figured prominently in the literary and intellectual life of New York. With their daughter Harriet, an ebullient 7-year-old, from whose flights of fancy and rhetoric her father has been known to borrow, they occupy a cooperative duplex apartment in mid-Manhattan, off Central Park. The Victorian décor, dominated by "an unauthenticated Burne-Jones" hanging above the fireplace, and the majestic proportions of the book-lined living room, with its 20-foot ceiling, recall the turn of the century, when the building was designed as a luxurious nest of studio apartments for nonstruggling artists.

"Our move from Boston to New York gave me a tremendous push," says Lowell. "Boston is all history and recollection; New York is ahead of one. Sympathetic spirits are a rarity elsewhere. Here there is a whole community of the arts, an endlessly stimulating fellowship . . . at times too stimulating. No one is too great for New York, and yet I grant there is something frightening about it."

He is asked to comment on a passage from his remarks at the Boston Arts Festival in 1960, when he was the honored poet: "Writing is neither transport nor a technique. My own owes everything to a few of our poets who have tried to write directly about what mattered to them, and yet to keep faith with their calling's tricky, specialized, unpopular possibilities for good workmanship. When I finished *Life Studies*, I was left hanging on a question mark. I am still hanging there. I don't know whether it is a death rope or a lifeline."

"Thankfully," he responds with the hint of a smile, "the lifeline seems to me both longer and stronger than I thought at that time."

He notes that he is feeling unusually fit, as his bronzed look confirms, after a summer in Castine, Me., where the Lowells have an old house on the

From The *New York Times Book Review,* October 4, 1964, p. 34+. ©1964 by The New York Times Company. Reprinted by permission.

Commons, a gift from his cousin Harriet Winslow. His weight—he has a tendency to gain—is down to 170 pounds, ideal for his 6-foot frame.

"In *Life Studies*," he continues, "I wanted to see how much of my personal story and memories I could get into poetry. To a large extent, it was a technical problem, as most problems in poetry are. But it was also something of a cause: to extend the poem to include, without compromise, what I felt and knew. Afterwards, having done it, I did not have the same necessity. My new book, *For the Union Dead*, is more mixed, and the poems in it are separate entities. I'm after invention rather than memory, and I'd like to achieve some music and elegance and splendor, but not in any programmatic sense. Some of the poems may be close to symbolism. After all, it's a bore to keep putting down just the things you know."

As Lowell talks, slumped in his chair until he is practically sitting on his spine, he knits his brow and stirs an invisible broth with his right index finger. The troubled blue eyes, intense and roving behind the thick glasses, rarely come to rest.

"The kind of poet I am was largely determined by the fact that I grew up in the heyday of The New Criticism, with Eliot's magical scrutiny of the text as a critical example. From the beginning I was preoccupied with technique, fascinated by the past, and tempted by other languages. It is hard for me to imagine a poet not interested in the classics. The task is to get something new into old forms, even at the risk of breaking them.

"So much of the effort of the poem is to arrive at something essentially human, to find the right voice for what we have to say. In life we speak with many false voices; occasionally, if we are lucky, we find a true one in our poems. A poem needs to include a man's contradictions. One side of me, for example, is a conventional liberal, concerned with causes, agitated about peace and justice and equality, as so many people are. My other side is deeply conservative, wanting to get at the roots of things, wanting to slow down the whole modern process of mechanization and dehumanization, knowing that liberalism can be a form of death too. In the writing of a poem all our compulsions and biases should get in, so that finally we don't know what we mean."

The contradictions of which Lowell speaks are present in his face and manner. The sensitive curved mouth contrasts with the jutting, fleshy chin; the nose is small, with wide circular nostrils; he is articulate, informed and positive, but his gestures are vague and rather endearingly awkward. With his friends he has an air of affectionate dependency, which makes him seem perpetually boyish, despite the 47 years, the grizzled hair, the deep parentheses etched at the corners of his mouth. He is knowing about fame and power, but no less knowing about his weaknesses. His ambition and pride are real, but so is his modesty. It would be hard to imagine another poet of comparable stature saying to his interviewer and meaning it, "I should be interviewing you," or prefacing a book of his poems with such a disarmingly candid note as the one that introduces *For the Union Dead:*

"I want to make a few admissions and disclosures. My poems on Hawthorne and Edwards draw heavily on prose sentences by their subjects. 'The Scream' owes everything to Elizabeth Bishop's beautiful, calm story, 'In the Village.' 'The Lesson' picks up a phrase or two from Rafael Alberti. 'Returning' was suggested by Giuseppe Ungaretti's 'Canzone.' 'The Public Garden' is a recasting and clarification of an old confusing poem of mine called 'David and Bathsheba in the Public Garden.' 'Beyond the Alps' is the poem I published in *Life Studies,* but with a stanza restored at the suggestion of John Berryman."

He has a great gift for friendship. No one is more generous than Robert Lowell in acknowledging his indebtedness to anybody who has ever helped him with a problem or with a poem.

"The poets who most directly influenced me," he says, "were Allen Tate, Elizabeth Bishop and William Carlos Williams. An unlikely combination! . . . but you can see that Bishop is a sort of bridge between Tate's formalism and Williams's informal art. For sheer language, Williams beats anybody. And who compares with him for aliveness and keenness of observation? I admire Pound but find it impossible to imitate him. Nor do I know how to use Eliot or Auden—their voice is so personal. Williams can be used, partly because he is somewhat anonymous. His poems are as perfect as anybody's, but they lead one to think of the possibility of writing them in different ways—for example, putting them into rhyme."

Lowell has had no secondary skills or hobbies to distract him from his absorption in literature. At 9:30 every morning, when he is in the city, he retires to his separate and private apartment on an upper floor of the building in which he lives. There he spends at least five or six hours reading and writing. He reads only three or four novels a year now, but is quite omnivorous in his capacity for literary periodicals and for books of poetry, criticism and history. He makes a point of returning regularly to the classics "with the aid of some sort of trot." Recently he has been reading Juvenal and Dante. Some of his scholarship is specifically designed to prepare him for his courses at Harvard, where he teaches two days a week. "I have had the advantage," he reflects, "of an independent income, which made it unnecessary for me to work for a living. I came to teaching voluntarily and quite late, having been unfit for it in my youth."

Lowell occupies himself tirelessly with literary evaluations, comparisons and ratings. "The modern poem of length that interests me most," he remarks, sweepingly, "is Pound's *Cantos,* the only long poem of the century that really comes off, even with all its flaws. One reason for my sustained interest in it is that it continues to puzzle me. In so many respects Pound remains a pre-Raphaelite figure, filled with nostalgia for the pure song of the troubadours and a lost pre-Renaissance innocence. What saved him as a poet was his bad politics, which got him involved in the contemporary world. The *Cantos* are not so good as Faulkner, but they are better than Hemingway and better than the work of any other novelist we've had since James. Dreiser's *American Tragedy,* which is comparable in scale, is humanly superior to the *Cantos,* but technically and stylistically inferior."

His taste for fine prose is as keen as his taste for verse. "As Pound said, poetry ought to be at least as well-written as prose. Furthermore, if you have sufficient control of the measure, you ought to be able to say anything in poetry that you can say in prose. The main difference between prose and poetry is a matter of technique: prose is written in paragraphs, poetry in lines. I am fascinated by the prose grip on things that somehow lets the music in and invites the noble splendor of a formal art. Swinburne's voice is dead because it's all music and no experience. Hardy owed a great deal to Swinburne, as we know from his elegy, but his grasp on reality put him out of Swinburne's class.

"Both Hardy and John Clare were clumsy but honest craftsmen who sometimes wrote remarkably well. Some of the intricate musical stanzas in Hardy have the solidity of a stone-mason's job. In an anthology that I was reading the other day I came across 'The Frigate Pelican' of Marianne Moore's with a sense of relief and liberation, not because it wasn't well-made, but because it was made differently, outside the groove of conventional poetics. It caused the other poems to wither. I am still tempted by metrical forms and continue to write them on occasion, but I am aware that meter can develop into a kind of paralysis. Sometimes I start regular and end irregular; sometimes the other way around."

With an accelerated stir of his finger, Lowell tries to sum up his argument on the relationship between prose and poetry. "In general, the poets of the last generation have lasted much better than the novelists. By way of illustration, contrast Williams with Thomas Wolfe. Yet the poets need the prose-writers and have a lot to learn from them. The style of a Flaubert or of a Faulkner affects the tradition of poetry as much as it affects the tradition of fiction. An ideal poetic language is more likely to resemble the art of Chekhov than that of Dylan Thomas. Maybe Thomas's language is too sonorous to be at the center of poetry. The best poets have an enormous respect for prose. After all, the great novelists of the 19th century make *Idylls of the King* seem frivolous. The supreme epic of the last 150 years is *War and Peace,* of the last 50 years, *Ulysses.*"

The conversation veers to the subject of poetic reputation. Lowell is without doubt the most celebrated poet in English of his generation. Almost from the beginning it seemed that he could do no wrong. Why? After several false starts and a deepening of the furrows in his brow, Lowell proposes a tentative reply:

"I can't really explain why that much attention has been paid to me. Looking back at *Lord Weary's Castle,* for example, my first full-length collection, I see it as out of the mainstream, a rather repellent, odd, symbolic Catholic piece of work. It may be that some people have turned to my poems because of the very things that are wrong with me. I mean the difficulty I have with ordinary living, the impracticability, the myopia. Seeing less than others can be a great strain. One has to learn how to live with one's limitations. I don't like to admit that my gift is for short pieces, but I'm better off knowing it."

The British critic, A. Alvarez, has recently paired Lowell with John Berryman as writers of "poetry of immense skill and intelligence which coped openly with the quick of their experience, experience sometimes on the edge of disintegration and breakdown. . . . Where once Lowell tried to externalize his disturbances theologically in Catholicism and rhetorically in certain mannerisms of language and rhythm, he is now . . . trying to cope with them nakedly, and without evasion."

Lowell does not try to skirt the issue, though it is difficult for him to discuss. "We are more conscious of our wounds," he ruminates, "than the poets before us, but we are not necessarily more wounded. Is Stevens or Eliot or Pound really any sadder at the heart or more vulnerable than Keats or Coleridge? The difference may be that modern art tries more deliberately to save the unsavable by giving it form. I am inclined to argue that it is better to be happy and kind than to be a poet. The truth is that no sort of life seems to preclude poetry. Poetry can come out of utterly miserable or disorderly lives, as in the case of a Rimbaud or a Hart Crane. But to make the poems possible a huge amount of health has to go into the misery."

Lowell finds the sources of his poems, variously, in a theme, an image, a musical phrase; sometimes in a prose passage or in another poem, preferably in a foreign language. The first draft is only a beginning. Only once did he ever complete a poem in a day. That was "The Tenth Muse," a poem about sloth! He makes a practice of showing his original draft to his poet friends, whose criticisms and suggestions he dutifully studies. A poem for him does not, as for Yeats, close shut with a click like a box. It only becomes less blurred. He does not believe in perfectibility. "In a way a poem is never finished. It simply reaches a point where it isn't worth any more alteration, where any further tampering is liable to do more harm than good. There are passages in all my books that make me wince, but I can't do anything with them. The worst grievance is the limitation inherent in any poet's character—the fact that Wordsworth, for example, can't be turned into Falstaff. That central limitation is far more serious than a few bad lines."

Suddenly, somewhat to his astonishment, Lowell is quite deeply involved in the theater. A trilogy of his plays, *The Old Glory*, now in rehearsal, will open at The American Place Theatre in New York on Oct. 26, under the direction of Jonathan Miller. The first two plays were suggested by Hawthorne and the last by Melville's "Benito Cereno." Together they cover a span of American history, from 1630 to 1805. "What they say about heroism, idealism, and violence," says Lowell, "is meant to apply to the present and to the future as well as to the past. *The Old Glory* is partly a tribute to that past and partly pure irony. My theme might be summed up in this paradox: we Americans might save the world or blow it up; perhaps we should do neither."

One of the satisfactions of writing for the theater, adds Lowell, with a laughing inflection, is that "you don't have to do all the work yourself." In the production of *The Old Glory* almost a hundred people are involved, and "it is they—particularly Jonathan—who make the original act of the imagination real."

Lowell is already at work on another play, having been commissioned by Lincoln Center to do an acting version of the Oresteia of Aeschylus, for production in the fall of 1965. During this past summer in Maine he completed the "Agamemnon," the first part of the trilogy. In the back of his head he has a play about Trotsky simmering.

At the door, where he offers a warm valedictory hand, Lowell stands for a moment surveying the pantheon of his friends and heroes whose photographs adorn the staircase wall. These cherished countenances, who are very much a part of the Lowell life and household, include—in so far as one remembers—T. S. Eliot, Ezra Pound, William Carlos Williams, Robert Frost, Boris Pasternak, John Crowe Ransom, Edmund Wilson, the Allen Tates, I. A. Richards, William Empson, Randall Jarrell, Flannery O'Connor and Elizabeth Bishop.

Exhausted as he is, at 2 in the morning, after more than five vehement hours of conversation, he is loth to let you go until the final resolving word has been spoken.

"You wouldn't write poetry unless you felt it had some chance of lasting. But if you get too concerned about posterity, you're in danger of becoming pompous and fraudulent. The poet needs to keep turning to something immediate and alive . . . something important, engaging, un-Olympian. It's a waste of time to dream about immortality, but it's important to try for a poem that continues to be good, even though you realize that it's somehow a mockery for a poem to last longer than you do.

"You write poetry without hoping to attract too much attention, and it would be foolish to aim for a great audience that doesn't exist. Most people have a contempt for poetry—it's so ineffectual—but there may be some envy mixed up in that reaction. Today 'poet' is a slightly laughable and glamorous word."

Michael Billington

Mr. Robert Lowell on T. S. Eliot and the Theatre

"Beautifully civil" was how someone described Robert Lowell's translation of *Phèdre*. The same words might be applied to the American poet himself. His manner is gracious and friendly, his appearance slightly suggestive of a don engrossed with problems of scholarship. But just as Lowell's poetry seems to have enormous reserves of strength under its usually calm surface, so the man himself can be unyielding on matters of principle, as his public actions have proved.

He is in London for the opening of his play, *Benito Cereno*, at the Mermaid tonight; and in the theatre foyer one morning this week surrounded by a small band of cleaners with mops and pails, he talked concisely and openly about his work. The Herman Melville short story from which he has adapted this particular play has always been one of his favourite books: he first read it as a student 30 years ago and he ranks it second only to *Moby Dick* in the Melville canon. In translating it to the stage, he has tried to keep faith with the original while adding a number of details: "An Argentinian writer, Borges, once said that you could tell the Koran was genuine because it didn't mention camels, whereas if you were translating it you would put the camels in. This happens with a dramatization. For instance, here, I've included a lot about the French Revolution not in the original. I've also put a lot of myself into the central character and I've disregarded exact historical chronology. If anyone wanted to check the text, he would probably find a network of tiny errors."

Between Melville and Lowell himself, however, one senses unusual affinities. Like the author of *Moby Dick*, Lowell seems to have the sea in his blood.

From The London *Times*, March 8, 1967, p. 10. Reprinted by permission of Times Newspapers Ltd.

"I grew up every summer by the sea and, as a boy I often went sailing. I've never sailed in a whaling boat, of course, but I wouldn't ever want to live far away from the sea." Issues that unconsciously stirred Melville are consciously present in his adapter: "Melville wrote his story on the eve of the Civil War and it came into his work in an intuitive, clairvoyant way. All kinds of things were in my mind when I wrote the play—the Civil Rights issue most of all." Finally, Melville had what Lowell calls "a feeling for operatic melodrama": and before sitting down to write his play, Lowell had been studying exactly that subject and attending hundreds of opera rehearsals.

To date, Lowell's work for the theatre has consisted entirely of adaptations and translations, but these obviously carry his own distinctive imprint. His next work, a new version of Aeschylus's *Prometheus,* will be twice as long as the original and applicable to our own age. "The story is of a guy chained to a rock, but it's what goes through his mind that's important. I didn't have to put in cigarette lighters or motor cycles to make it up to date. His thoughts all come out of our world." But Lowell would also like to write plays about twentieth-century figures, and he mentions Trotsky and Malcolm X as examples. The difficulty, he feels, would be partly one of idiom and partly the weight of documentary evidence: as he says, Shakespeare had only Holinshed and Plutarch to work from when writing his histories.

Although *Benito Cereno* has an undeniably poetic feel to it, Lowell seems a little wary of the term "poetic drama." "For me, poetic drama means anything non-naturalistic or heightened. The sort of thing that Christopher Fry does I'm not interested in. I find it better to write in paragraphs than lines because one can sustain an idea that way." Eliot's suggestion that there are certain states of being that can achieve theatrical expression only in verse does not strike a chord with him. "I knew Eliot well. His essays on Elizabethan dramatists were almost my introduction to drama. But I wish that he himself had tried to use a more gaudy style, something more like the Elizabethans themselves. In trying to throw out the purple passages, he sometimes threw out the poetry as well."

When the question of modern American poetry is raised, Lowell finds little to cheer. "I see oceans of competence in every kind of style. There have never been so many competent people writing poetry. But there needs to be more personality—not just technique or the imitation of something better. Most of the poets I admire at the moment are women—Sylvia Plath, for instance." Lowell himself combines writing poetry with three months' academic work every year. "My old friend, Randall Jarrell, once said that he liked teaching so much that, if he were rich enough, he'd pay to be a teacher. I don't go so far as that but I do like it. Besides a poet can get awfully full of himself if he works alone."

No one could accuse Robert Lowell of being full of himself: there is about him a hint of that "triumphant diffidence" he once praised in a friend. At the same time, he has not been afraid to stand publicly by his principles: he was gaoled in wartime as a conscientious objector and he refused an invitation to the White House because of his feelings about Vietnam. About this, he says reasonably: "It's all to the good if a gesture of protest can be symbolic—it helps if it's more than verbal, anyway. But there's no reason why a poet shouldn't simply write poetry like Herrick or de la Mare if he wants to." In its combination of tolerance with strong personal convictions this says a lot about the spirit of Robert Lowell.

Richard Gilman

"Life Offers No Neat Conclusions"

I talked to Robert Lowell on Easter Sunday. Half a block away from the large, beautifully unmodern apartment in the West Sixties where he lives with his wife Elizabeth Hardwick and their 11-year-old daughter Harriet, Central Park was jumping with hippies, yippies and others of the disaffected and affected, gathered for an impromptu spring be-in. A few blocks south, the Coliseum was holding the first International Motorcycle show, and Columbus Circle was ringed with shining cycles whose leather-clad owners were being amiably stared at by Indian-clad hippies.

Lowell, who is 51, and I talked at first about early America, the period from the origins to the early 19th century, the span in which his trilogy, *The Old Glory,* is set. "Endecott and the Red Cross," the first play in the sequence but the last to be staged, takes place in a colonial settlement in Massachusetts in the 1630's. It has been playing at the American Place Theater since April 18 although, in keeping with its usual practice, the church-theater has asked critics to hold off their reviews until this Tuesday.

The three plays, which obviously can be staged separately, do, however, have a unity, which Lowell regards as roughly having to do with certain basic American experiences, more particularly New England experiences, whose

From The *New York Times,* May 5, 1968, pp. 1, 5. © 1968 by The New York Times Company. Reprinted by permission.

effects and implications run through all our history. When I mentioned the flag as a unifying symbol, he said that he didn't think too much should be made of that, since it was there largely for "harmonic repetition." I then remarked that it seemed to me that what really binds the three plays together is their dealing with certain generally ignored tensions in American experience, specifically the tensions and antinomies rising from the hidden painfulness of our origins, the contradictions of our freedom and self-definition, the losses that all aggressive gains entail. He nodded in agreement, his long, rather quizzical, gray-haired, civilized head bobbing slowly up and down.

"Endecott" has been considerably revised from the version I'd read and also seen in a staged reading several years ago. "I've shortened [lengthened?] it, for one thing," Lowell said, "and I think it's more actable now." This led us to a wide-ranging discussion of the present-day theater, of what constitutes the dramatic, the role of language, the question of whether the stage is as boring today as many people say: the sort of conversation, in short, it would be difficult to imagine having with an "established," institutionalized playwright.

Lowell said: "I know much less about plays than you do. I don't go to the theater very much . . . and I mostly like old plays. The great moments I remember are a Chekhov powerfully done, or an Ibsen . . . something like that. The rest is reading plays. You know, I find fragments more interesting usually than whole plays. Plots are boring anyway. We all hate the sort of play where one thing leads to another and everything is drawn tight."

I said that most good playwrights didn't care very much about plots, and that in fact he had taken his from Hawthorne and Melville. "Yes, using Hawthorne and Melville spared me a lot of work and gave me confidence that something was there. Of course, Shakespeare is the great example of borrowing plots. You know, recently I read *Macbeth,* skipping all the places where he or his wife don't speak. What I found was that it would have made a great poem, one of the greatest, with all those plot elements removed. But at the same time I think that to write a 'poetic' play now is death—all that emotion *pumped* into the theater."

I mentioned Cocteau's distinction between poetry *of* the theater and in it, and he nodded once again in agreement that the theater had its own poetry which certainly wasn't a matter of formal verse. "That's when you get Christopher Fry," he said, to which I added, "or Maxwell Anderson."

We talked then about the "new" theater, Off Off Broadway and its environs, happenings, mixed-media events and so on. "I'm not very much in touch with the new theater," Lowell said, "although I can't stand naturalistic theater, the usual thing, either. I think the new movements are perfectly legitimate, but as a word-man I can't be interested in anything that wants to do without language or restrict it so heavily. To me words are all-important, and you're giving up a lot, I think, when you give up words or give up using them well."

We agreed that the impulse against texts, against the sovereignity of language on the stage, was part of larger cultural and esthetic change, something about which Marshall McLuhan has, it seemed to me, said useful if also muddying things. Lowell spoke of having met McLuhan and liked him, and when I remarked that many writers I knew, or whose comments on McLuhan I'd read, regarded him with something close to fury or dread, he replied, "Oh, no, I find his ideas rather dull, not a menace. I remember thinking of him as a huge machine that could turn anything into anything else without regard to quality."

As to the position of language in drama, where it still mostly held its own, we agreed that, like poetry, drama has its own nonverbal element, a reality *beneath* the words. In a piece like "Marat/Sade" the words have very little importance, he said, but the dramatic occasion works. His own plays are written "carefully but plainly" and he knows that "a really good production would be better than any reading." But though they're essentially verbal, he would want them to be seen for the "nonverbal element in them."

I told him I thought his own plays were closer, for all their seeming traditionalism, to the works of certain experimental playwrights than they were, say to Arthur Miller's. "Yes," he replied, after meditating for a few moments (conversations with Lowell always contain these silences, good opportunities for the other party, if he wants them, to find out what he himself thinks), "this business of naturalistic plays: life doesn't offer such neat conclusions."

From here we went off into politics, which doesn't offer neat conclusions either. Lowell had recently returned from Wisconsin, where he had accompanied Senator Eugene McCarthy on the latter's campaigning. I asked him when and how he had met McCarthy. "I do most things accidentally," he said, "although the accidents are in character. A couple of years ago my wife was preparing a piece on senators for The New York Review. McCarthy was one of the few we were able to meet. I liked him from the start. It turned out he knew friends of mine from Minnesota—J. F. Powers and other writers—but more important, I felt a temperamental affinity between us. Oh, I don't mean we're alike—there are lots of differences—but we share certain attitudes and values.

"I like his humor. It mostly has to do with political jokes, but they're honest jokes, and they're connected with a deeper vein of seriousness."

I asked him to give me an example and he told me about a quip McCarthy had made at a luncheon at Harvard two years ago. The lunch was an informal occasion in which students could meet public men, and Lowell, who was teaching a seminar there, dropped in. Someone asked McCarthy what he thought of George Romney and Charles Percy as Presidential possibilities, to which he replied, "You know, America has given two original religions to the world. The Mormons believe what isn't true, and the Christian Scientists don't believe what is true."

(I refrained from telling Lowell of my strong feeling of having heard this before, mostly because I liked the fact that McCarthy had used the joke, so that its possible lack of originality didn't trouble me.)

His own role in the McCarthy campaign, Lowell went on to say, had nothing directly political about it. When I said that it seemed to me that he was there simply as human contact, to give McCarthy that kind of support, he agreed, adding that the men whom McCarthy, like any political person, was surrounded by were rather narrow and lacking in wit and humor.

He is probably going to accompany McCarthy during the California campaign, he said. When I asked him about Bobby Kennedy, he said that Kennedy would be his choice if McCarthy didn't make it. "I know him fairly well, and he's a lot better than he seems to a lot of people."

We talked then about the role of the writer in politics. "This whole peace business," Lowell said. "When your private experience converges on the nation's experience, you feel you have to do something. Writers have to act publicly sometimes from private experience. . . . You know, when you have relations, as a writer, with public men, there has to be equality. I went to John Kennedy's inauguration, but before going I sent him a copy of one of my books of poetry. When I was introduced to him he gave me the kind of compliment that indicated he'd really read the book, so I said to him, 'You're the first President who's treated your peers as equals.'

"This kind of equality—it's an ideal to be aspired to by both writers and public persons."

The afternoon was dying. We talked then about his writing again, about the mysteries of decision and procedure in the making of poems and plays. I mentioned Hebbel's rather wonderful statement that the secret of dramatic art lay in presenting the necessary in the form of the accidental. Lowell nodded vigorously. "That's it," he said. "You're free to pick up anything and put it in, and if it's right it points through to some deep meaning. I'm always happy when I toss something in and it works."

Outside, as evening came on, the hippies and yippies were still trying to toss something in, but despite all my sympathy I didn't think it seemed to be working.

D. S. Carne-Ross

Conversation with Robert Lowell

Thanks to Robert Lowell, poetic translation retains much of the importance which Ezra Pound won back for it. Lowell's translations are altogether unlike Pound's, though without that example they might never have been written. And yet like Pound, and like Pope, he presents the case of a poet of great originality who is continually reworking other men's poetry. Pound, by a kind of inspired ventriloquism, almost disappears into the author he is translating. But for his name at the head of the page, would we know that *The Seafarer, Cathay,* and the *Classic Anthology* were from the same pen? Lowell, although he believes he has never translated a poem he could have written himself, is almost always unmistakably present in his translations. And the more intensely he engages with the original, the more Lowellian the accent and the style. He strains to the utmost George Steiner's definition of poetic translation as "the writing of a poem . . . which can be read and responded to independently but which is not ontologically complete." He strains it, but he does not break it. We read his translations—and "imitations"—inadequately if we take them simply as new poems by Robert Lowell.

He has no "method." The same flexible intelligence that informs the original poems is at work in the translations. Each text requires a different approach. In the versions from Heine or Montale in *Imitations,* he gave himself a good deal of elbow room; the Juvenal and the Dante in *Near the Ocean* are done at close range. When I went to see him, he was busy with Mandelstam again, trying by slight changes of diction and word order to turn the literal versions he was using into formal verse. Yet he describes his *Prometheus Bound,* produced recently at Yale and soon to appear in London, as "derived from Aeschylus," a highly personal adaptation of the Greek original. I began with a question about *Prometheus:*

I don't know if this is unreasonable or imperceptive, but when I opened The New York Review *and found that your* Prometheus *was in prose, I was rather disappointed. I had counted on its being in verse.*

I no longer know the difference between prose and verse. In *The Old Glory,* the first and third plays, *Endecott* and *Benito Cereno,* are in free verse—that is, there is no scansion, the lines are of varying length. And the middle play is in four-foot lines. Well, the three sound more or less the same. I remember

From *Delos,* I (1968), 165-75. Reprinted by permission of the author.

my friend Randall Jarrell suggested to me it would have been better if *Benito* had been printed as prose—not changing a word but printing it in paragraphs rather than lines. And quite likely he was right, but it seemed to make very little difference. I happened to write it in lines, but if it had been printed as prose probably no one would have been able to tell.

Actors turn verse into prose anyway.

I'm sure I could have printed *Prometheus* in free-verse lines and then everyone would say it's poetry. It's very queer that change, but the kind of poetry I'm interested in for the stage would have the advantages of prose. I didn't even want to worry about line length when I was doing *Prometheus* but be perfectly free to be prolix and to elaborate as much as I wanted without any metrical restrictions.

Do you feel now that the verse form of your Phaedra *isn't really suitable for the stage?*

It has never been done well. I think it was a sort of tour de force putting *Phaedra* into heroic couplets. But I don't know what to do with that material.

It's a question of formal equivalents, isn't it? With a language as near to us as French, you've got a chance of creating something that is pretty close to Racine's couplets or Baudelaire's quatrains. But there's no living equivalent for Greek verse. So what do you do? Different people try different things. Some translators use the twelve-syllable line, but that doesn't work at all—it's not a true English meter. Or there's the six-stress line that people like Richmond Lattimore use for Homer. I don't know what you think about that.

I admire Lattimore's translations a lot—they are just the opposite of what I am trying to do. I once taught the *Iliad* in Greek, with a Greek professor, at Iowa, and we used Lattimore as a trot. I was amazed to discover that each line of Lattimore's was the same as in Homer. He was actually closer than the Samuel Butler prose translation that we also used.

But he sacrifices so much.

You can't possibly call Lattimore's *Iliad* great poetry. He has invented a kind of literal verse translation, more literal than any in English, I think. He avoids the usual translator's clichés, but it's dry and unmusical. All the same, I admire it very much. When I did a passage from the *Iliad* in my book *Imitations,* I used his translation and the Greek very carefully and tried to make mine—not a critique of his, I tried to do something very different in blank verse.

I wonder if what you want from him isn't simply the closeness. When you read a translation, aren't you looking for something you could do over and improve? In a sense, if a translation is bad it's all the more stimulating.

I used his translation of *Agamemnon* for a cut version I did. I was trying there to be very brief and rapid. I think mine is about thirty-five pages shorter than Aeschylus and much shorter than Lattimore.

Yes, I can see that Lattimore is useful to you.

There are translations which interest me, like Lattimore's, or Binyon's *Divina Commedia,* that are more difficult, in a way, than the original. Yet they're very accurate. I think Lattimore is probably harder to follow than Homer if you are any good at Greek. And Binyon is much harder than Dante if you know Italian. Binyon is quite accurate, but he is crippled by the *terza rima* in English.

But don't you feel that Binyon is trying for something Lattimore isn't? I mean, he tries to follow the movement, the rhythmical movement, of Dante's lines.

But I don't think it's exactly great poetry in Binyon. It's something in-between poetry. Its metrics. It's distinguished metrics, but it's very dry compared to Dante. A work of genius, but not very readable poetry. Of course the great episodes in Dante are so great that an honest poetic translator is bound to have something that sounds like pretty good poetry, but I feel Binyon's diction is cramped and knotted. I found that I was constantly looking at the Italian to discover what Binyon was saying and then I found he was saying what the Italian was saying, but he was saying it in the language of about 1910—like minor Robert Bridges. . . .

Binyon's diction is old-fashioned, sometimes deliberately archaic, but the meter isn't. For instance, he rhymes a stressed and an unstressed syllable in a way that is not traditional.

Would you admit that something could be wonderful metrics without being particularly important poetry?

Kipling?

But I think his is real poetry. It's the opposite—it's too open and easy to understand. Of course he's a much better poet than Binyon.

Kipling is a great verse-writer—I believe that is what one says.

But Binyon isn't a good verse-writer the way Kipling is. He's good metrics.

This is a promising category. Can you think of other writers who fit into it? Some of Swinburne, perhaps, is interesting mainly for its metrical movement.

Well, take Auden, for example—perhaps the best poet writing in America. His *Age of Anxiety* seems to me a masterpiece of metrics, but it stops at that point. Auden's great poems are everything—they're metrics *and* inspiration. *The Age of Anxiety* is an incredible tour de force of alliterative poetry, but somehow it's not very interesting beneath that. Remember Eliot's joke about Milton, that you read him once for the sense and once for the sound. Well, you can read *The Age of Anxiety* for its meter with great joy, but somehow the meter exists on its own.

It's a poem I read quite often. Maybe I read it for the meter. I'm not sure, I shall have to think about this. At any rate, it suggests another question. Given the enormous part that meter—and rhythm—play in our experience of poetry, I wonder what exactly happens when one translates not from the original but from a prose crib, as I believe you have done. I mean, what is being translated? In a crib, the sensuous body of poetry is missing, everything contributed by meter and rhythm and the sound and shape of words is missing, and all that remains is the "sense," the meaning. What exactly is it that the translator, in this case, translates?

Well, I have translated I think in five or six different ways. With Baudelaire, for instance, all that I had were bad verse translations, not prose crib. I did my own translation and as I read French fairly well, the text was very available to me. When I did Pasternak, I didn't have prose cribs either. I had rather uninspired verse translations and I tried to make them into English poems. In other cases I have had absolutely accurate prose versions and sometimes they were more important to me than the originals. There you are trying to put flesh on some kind of dry bones.

Do you get someone to read you the poem in the originals?

No, it just bores me to hear a language I don't understand. People have sometimes read me Russian and so forth. But the worst Russian poet would sound like the best, I couldn't tell. You could get the meter, but I don't think sound effects are transferable from one language to another. I know what Baudelaire's sound effects are like and I try to get something else in English.

Yet in trying for something else, you have written lines that are pure Baudelaire in English—
            this lying trickle swollen with your tears,
for instance, from "The Swan." That's the wonderful thing about some of those versions. The Baudelaire, and the Montale, I think—those are the two where there is the most intimate contact between you and the original.

Baudelaire was a real metrist. It was a delight to me just trying to write the quatrains. I wrote and rewrote them. The Montale comes out as free verse in my translations and there was none of that problem there. There I rewrote to improve the diction and make it more alive. I had complete freedom—nothing *had* to go in. The Baudelaire was very hard for me, just to rhyme. I first did them in blank verse, then tried to rhyme them. I really did countless versions, shifting, changing lines. I wanted a rather elegant surface. I have a feeling that Baudelaire in French sounds a little like the best parts of Pope—where Pope is being dramatic, as in the passage on the death of the Duke of Buckingham, a rather Baudelairian subject.

What do you think about the sheer amount of translation that is being pro-duced today? It seems to me that a flourishing, let alone a great, period of translation presupposes a particular relation to foreign literature. You may need a lot of translation, as in sixteenth-century England; there was the sense that Plutarch and Ovid and Montaigne had got to be put into English. To some extent this is true of today. Or you may have the Augustan situation, the sense that England has "arrived" and is now in a comparable cultural situation to ancient Rome. Pope's imitations of Horace are so good partly because they are so confident. The Goths have been defeated, Pope is living in his villa at Twickenham just as Horace lived on his Sabine farm, a great minister like Lord Burlington is his friend just as Maecenas was Horace's friend, he can meet Horace eye to eye. That situation obviously doesn't exist today. What is it, do you think—apart from the obvious demand, which mostly produces run-of-the-mill stuff—that leads so many poets to translate now?

I think there is much more stir of poetic translation now than there was when I was in college in the thirties. I'm not sure why. I'll just give my own case—that may be more accurate. When I began writing poetry, studying Pound and his translations and Ford Madox Ford who held very similar views, I read Ford's *The March of World Literature* which made it all sound attrac-tive and I remember something he said to me. I was going from Harvard to Kenyon College. I had, as a sophomore, been majoring in English at Harvard, but I had decided to change to Classics. Ford said to me in a rather superior but kind tone, "Yes, of course you should, otherwise you'll cut yourself off from humanity." He meant not just the Classics but all literature. I think we have the feeling of discovery of what we lack. Someone like Neruda has something that no North American poet has. So has Pasternak, so has some quite small-scale poet from, say, Sweden. We have a limited amount of energy to absorb these things, but we're trying to. Each person likes someone differ-ent.

And it has something to do with politics, with the terrifying world situation, with the way we can go from one country to another, the way one country can destroy another country. This is something unprecedented in human history. We have never known so many languages, we have never spread ourselves as a power into so many countries. Countries have never been so much in contact, politically and militarily.

Yes, and there's something else now, a kind of poetic koiné *or* lingua franca *which means that poets in different countries are writing in similar ways even though they don't know each other's works. This openness of poets to poetry in other places seems to me new. I mean, Tennyson and Browning didn't translate Leopardi and Baudelaire. And even in the thirties, Auden and Spender were not translating.*

But Pound was, and Eliot was very strong on different literatures. And Matthew Arnold knew Leopardi very well. He knew how Leopardi differed from other Italians and how Heine differed from German Romantics, and of course he knew French well. His whole point was that you couldn't understand Wordsworth if you couldn't understand Goethe and Leopardi and Heine. They all had inspirations that Wordsworth lacked.

Certainly, but this was part of a cultural program, part of his struggle to educate the English and make them less provincial. I was thinking of something different: the way a poet from Peru, say, can feel instinctively how a poet thousands of miles away works, even if he hardly understands his language.

It's always a difficult bridge, particularly when two poets don't know each other's language very well, understanding the niceties of another man's culture.

But somehow the bridges are built, more now than in the past.

Yes, I don't know why. But I'm very interested in this. I read a lot and stumble away in other languages and I can name about six poets I know at all well in other countries. Yves Bonnefoy in French, Voznesenskii in Russian, Miroslav Holub in Czech, and there are a lot more that I admire. Enzensberger I have met and enjoyed, but I know him very slightly. I was at Expo and there was a poetry conference which like all such things was very tedious, but the best part, for me, was talking with the poets from France. We had to talk French and listen to French and this is very painful to me, but after a while with a little wine it got rather pleasant and you felt that something came over. There is something generic about poets that is hard to define, but they're not like a group of economics professors or philosophers or even novelists—even though you'd much rather meet a good economist than a bad poet.

There's another point I wanted to put to you. What do you think is the difference between the translation of a poet in the public domain—like Horace, say, or Baudelaire—a poet the reader already possesses, and like Mandelstam who most readers don't yet possess? What does the reader do with a translation of a new poet in a language he doesn't know? Can he read it as a translation? Is he not bound to approach it as an original poem?

Well, there's a great charm in doing a first—or a near first, nobody ever seems to do a real first. But you do an almost first Mandelstam, say, and that's wonderful. A lot of the best translations ever done are firsts—I suppose *Cathay* was largely a first. Part of the excitement is that it's news, but if it's only that, and most firsts are just news, then they soon fade as poetry.

A lot of the Russian translation that appears is just that. They depend on the politically exciting fact that we can talk to the Russians now.

Well, nine-tenths of the competent translations being done today in verse, to say nothing of the incompetent ones, are of no value except as news. They get the thing over for the moment and that's very valuable, but there will be much better translations later on.

Do you agree that this sort of translation ought to be pretty close, whereas with a poet in the public domain you can afford to be as free as you like because the reader can set the original beside the translation? This is Baudelaire, that is Lowell. He can see what's happening.

You can also argue that an unknown poet like Mandelstam needs even greater freedom to be made as interesting in English as he is in Russian.

Yes, that's the line I personally am inclined to take.

I think that's perfectly valid. No one should inflict on the market a long, dull collected Pasternak done by Professor X in meter that is very bad, very uninspired English poetry. That does nothing for Pasternak, or next to nothing.

Ideally, there should be three tiers: the original, a poet's translation, then a literal trot. We need all three. This is one of the things I want to do in Delos.

There could be a law, though I don't really believe in it, that almost nobody would be allowed to do a verse translation of poetry. He'd have to do an accurate prose trot. And these trots are usually better poetry than the professor's or even the minor poet's poetic translation of a masterpiece.

I'd certainly prefer George Kay's translations of Montale if they had been in prose rather than verse.

I checked the changes of phrasing when he turned his Penguin prose into verse and two-thirds of the time they were worse. I still think his versions are awfully good, but I wish he had printed them as prose.

There is something here that has a kind of pathos to it. Innumerable people for some reason want to be poets, and the only way they can be poets is by doing Virgil or Pasternak into English verse, and it's very bad, very dull poetry. Then every so often there is an Edward FitzGerald who does an inspired translation—a man who isn't a very interesting poet except when he's translating.

Yes, but he wrote some original poetry, even if it isn't up to much. Is there any case of a man who's written no original verse at all coming up with a fine verse translation? It's particularly afflicting with the Classics. A professor who has never written a line of verse in his life seems to think he has a professional right to translate great Greek or Latin poetry just because he knows the language.

Most of them can't write prose either. . . . I remember a wonderful crack of Randall Jarrell's about translation. He said nobody thinks that some professor of Lithuanian could have written *Anna Karenina,* but everyone thinks he is the ideal man to translate it. All the same, there must be a hundred people in America who could do a readable translation of Tolstoy. But they couldn't do Pushkin, probably no one could do Pushkin unless they did it in prose the way Edmund Wilson did "The Bronze Horseman." But then he's a prose writer.

I wonder if we are not putting verse and prose translation too much in different categories, demanding inspiration from the one and accepting mere competence—"accuracy"—in the other. The verse translator is allowed to take certain liberties in order to get his text off the ground, but the prose translator is still stuck with this word-for-word thing. People complain of Scott-Moncrief that he hasn't got this word right or the exact sense of that phrase. Only the worst kind of pedant approaches verse translation in this way now.

Scott-Moncrief's Proust is at the least an English masterpiece.

I agree—or at least I think I do.

And it's no worse written than George Eliot. Another English masterpiece.

No comment, but one final point. One thing that translation can do is let the original language violate English just a little in order to bring something into English which wasn't there before. The only defect I see in your masterful way of translating is that you sometimes simply take possession of the original and dominate it. I am particularly interested in those places—I think

they're most frequent in your Baudelaire—where you let the original language impose itself for a moment on your English. For instance, in your version of "La servante au grand coeur," you have the line
> The dead, the poor dead, they have their bad hours.

It seems to me there is something marginally un-English, something rhetorical in the repetition of "the dead, the poor dead," which has come from Baudelaire's French rhetoric. The same thing happens in your version of "Le Cygne" where the swan screams at the heavens:

> Its heart was full of its blue lakes, and screamed:
> "Water, when will you fall? When will you burst,
> oh thunderclouds?"

An English swan, even a Yeatsian Irish swan, couldn't scream at the heavens in this grand way without a touch of absurdity. This belongs to the Latin rhetoric of emotion which you have somehow made us accept in English.

I think you have raised the most important question of the morning. In a way the whole point of translating—of my translation, anyway—is to bring into English something that didn't exist in English before. I don't think I've ever done a translation of a poem I could have written myself. I wouldn't know how to answer this point. For instance, when I do a Victor Hugo poem: it's written in a way I wouldn't dare write in English myself, yet I admire it very much. To a certain extent that's true of everyone I have translated. It's a great grief to me that I can't write my original poems in the styles I have used in my translation. I wish I could use Baudelaire and write a poem like "The Swan."

Isn't your poem "The Flaw" very Baudelairian? The way you use the scene, the way the theme is dissolved in, or presented through, the scene. I feel you couldn't have written it but for your work with Baudelaire.

Well, there's a bit of "Cimetière Marin" there too.

Yes, but I'm sure Baudelaire is behind it.

I can't tell, but I hope something has rubbed off. You can't go about it too deliberately. I felt this doing Juvenal—which most people criticize as being too close to Juvenal. I just wish I could write an original poem like that with historical portraits like his Sejanus and Hannibal. I'd feel like the greatest poet alive if I could do Lincoln that way.

Do what Johnson did with it, you mean, and take the poem over completely, putting American figures in the place of Juvenal's Roman ones?

Well, Johnson's is one of the great poems in English. Though I'd have to say that his use of English history is much less interesting than Juvenal's use of Roman history. He's much less soaked in it. You can hardly exaggerate what good poetry his portraits of Charles XII and Wolsey are, but on the whole you don't feel Johnson had much interest in history or knew much about it. Wolsey isn't a concrete person as Sejanus is, and he shouldn't be. That wasn't the way Johnson wrote.

He's more interested in the cultural parallels, perhaps, than in the characters themselves.

Again, "The Vanity of Human Wishes" has this slight defect—which I suppose makes it a great minor poem: the fact that the framework doesn't quite fit. Eighteenth-century London wasn't as awful as Juvenal's Rome, it was nothing like as murderous as the Rome of the emperors Juvenal wrote about, which in many ways is closer to us now, and yet he's forced to say that it was. This makes him slightly off key. On the other hand, Johnson did something much greater than I did in the way of transforming the poem. While I just try to give an accurate, eloquent photograph of the original, he did something much more avant-garde.

You mentioned the closeness of your Juvenal. In most of the versions in the second half of Near the Ocean *you keep nearer the original than you have usually done in the past. I wonder how far this is an attempt to make your translations complement, or balance, the original poems—which they couldn't do if they were already as nearly original poems by Robert Lowell as some of the versions in* Imitations. *In the preface you suggest that the two parts somehow match each other, though you don't quite know how. A number of obvious cross references seem to support this—like the similar risks of taking a walk in ancient Rome or in New York's Central Park.*

That would seem true except for the fact that the translations were written a year or so before. No, I don't know why but I felt you just couldn't be very original with Juvenal—or with Dante. On the other hand, two of the Horaces, the second and the third, are quite changed, and the Góngora and Quevedo work in about the same way as the versions in *Imitations*.

But on the whole you do keep closer to the texts in this book.

Maybe I felt ragged by people telling me I wasn't close enough in my imitations.

Do the critics annoy you?

No, it just seemed interesting to try to be more accurate.

What do you feel about the question of mistakes? Pound is deliberately very arrogant here. I fancy he refuses to look up words in the dictionary because he doesn't want his image of the poem to be sullied by what professors claim the words to mean.

I'd just as soon do a completely inaccurate translation again. Some of the versions in this book are in meter and some are not; and meter has something to do with accuracy. A metrical one may turn out more accurate, for some queer reason. It fascinates you, this sort of mosaic-work, transferring pebble by pebble into meter. Or meter may make you much more inaccurate—just the effort to handle it at all well in English. I took easy meters here: blank verse for Juvenal, two-rhyme *terza rima* for Dante. I wouldn't want to translate in any one way.

V. S. Naipaul

Et in America ego

LOWELL: When I went to school in New England and talked to people, it would have been death to them to admit mine was a famous name.

NAIPAUL: *Do you think it was because this linked you more closely to the old world: the fact that your family has been in America much longer?*

LOWELL: It would seem to make you less close to the old world and more provincial. New England does mean this one peculiar thing. I was reading somewhere of a student of Leavis, now a professor, who wrote a book saying that in 1800 Boston wasn't one of the more advanced American cities culturally. It was way behind Philadelphia, and even New York. But somehow by about 1830 the other cities didn't exist for a while—and I mean by 'Boston,' not only Boston itself, but Cambridge and Concord and New England in general, and people like James and Melville, who came from other places to New England. So it was one of the great moments of the 19th

From *The Listener*, LXXXII (September 4, 1969), 302-4. Reprinted by permission of the journal and the authors.

century. You can hardly walk through Boston, even though it has been re-
built, and not stumble on something that suggests at least 1800, or the
mid-19th century, 1870 or so. You go to New York, nothing. Nothing seems
to have been here 20 years ago: much *has,* yet it seems to have lost all
significance. That troubles me in New York, and New York and London, I
sometimes think, are one city. You see the same literary people, sometimes
literally the same people. But when you go to Boston there is a past everywhere. It doesn't exist here. I think that's ghastly about New York.

*—You have this reputation for being something of a rebel, someone who has
rebelled against his New England background. The actual rebellion, perhaps,
wasn't a very conscious one, but a matter of self-discovery?*

LOWELL: Self-discovery. But I didn't find the culture I was born in very
nourishing, quite aside from my relations with my parents. I felt I was born in
a kind of illiterate culture, a kind of decadence, and I was just very unhappy
anyway. I probably wanted to go away and fish and do various things I wasn't
supposed to do. Then when it came to writing, this feeling of getting away
from it continued. But I really think the place had lost its seriousness, its
imagination, and if you wanted to be a writer you couldn't be a conventional
New Englander.

—You felt the centre had shifted to New York perhaps?

LOWELL: No. I don't know what New York is. New York's a much more
exciting city than Boston. It's a Jewish city: about a third of the city is
Jewish and the talent is Jewish, all the most able people here are Jewish. New
York is much better than anything we have in New England, or even in the
South, which is much stronger. It's a very difficult thing for Jews and for
Gentiles to float this culture, and now Negroes are coming into it. I don't
think anyone should be very dogmatic about what's good and what's bad in
these various strains that go into New York, but the New York I know best is
Jewish New York. Most of my friends are Jewish, and the people I've learned
most from, and that I like best, in New York are Jewish. It's quite strange
that this tiny little minority should have such talent, and isn't anyway typical
of Jews, I think, through history.

*—You say you've left New England and you've had to penetrate the New
York literary world, which is now a mainly Jewish world. Do you feel that
you have submerged your special regional identity in something larger which
might be called American?*

LOWELL: America with a capital A I find a very hard thing to realize. It's
beyond any country, it's an empire. I feel very bitter about it, but pious, and
baffled by it. You know, if you're standing in cold water, you wish the whole

world was steaming. Living in America, I wish my own section of America—New England—were a small provincial country like Scotland, with its own capital and even customs barriers. Then it occurs to me how deadly it would be to have to live in Boston, the capital of that country, though Boston would be more lively if it were like Amsterdam, the head of a small country. But it's going to be a toothless little country, that can't throw a plastic bomb into Buffalo, or have sort of Rubens rapes of Buffalo women and carry them back to Worcester and Boston. But I think all little countries in Europe are better off than my New England. America now is not a country—it's something much larger. The melting pot's worked all too well: people have melted into one another.

—From the outside, one is aware of certain people in America with reputations, and one vaguely comes here expecting they'll be much more enmeshed in the life of the country than one finds them to be.

LOWELL: There's an equally great danger of getting too enmeshed in these things and talking baloney about things you know nothing about. The country's cause-mad. Every day letters come to me to sign—some foolish thing or unfoolish thing I know nothing about. But I once had a queer personal experience that I'd like to get straight. It was a time when Churchill, Brendan Bracken and Roosevelt met and said: we intend to burn something, and ruthlessly destroy, and we're saturating Hamburg and the northern German cities, the civilian population. They announced their policy of unconditional surrender. It seemed to me that we were doing just what the Germans were doing. I was a Roman Catholic at the time, and we had a very complicated idea of what was called "the unjust war." It is obviously a possibility that there may be two kinds of wars and one merges into the other. But this policy seemed to be clearly unjust. So I refused to go to the army and was sent to jail. I spent about five months in jail and mopped floors. Then I was paroled and was free to write. After that I felt that you weren't getting beyond your depth in protesting unjust wars.

—It's very strange because writers have been involved in so many causes and have contributed so much. Yet at the same time there does persist this old romantic idea of the writer as a man who is far away from the world.

LOWELL: I think that poets—and this probably holds for any artist—must be removed and they must be gregarious. I'd rather use "gregarious" than "engaged" as the opposite of "removed." You won't have anything to write about if you don't see people. A novelist particularly needs people, but even a poet needs a good deal. It's very hard to tell what combination is right and no combination is right as a category of what everybody who wants to write should follow.

—And so you came to the conclusion that the poet, like the novelist, had to be both in and out of the world. And you took this even further to the point of massive political intervention.

LOWELL: I think the arts are connected with power in a peculiar way, but it's an oblique way, and often comes when the power has faded. The great period of Italian painting, somehow, is a period not of power but of efficiency. It is no accident that Florence was the Pittsburgh of its day when the great Florentine painting came. You wouldn't call that very great power, as power goes. Still, it was there, and it's interesting that the great Spanish and Dutch periods more or less corresponded with their country's power and they tend to be best when that power is fading.

—Most Americans greet the visitor with the statement that it's all falling apart. Very, very quickly. But if one probes more deeply, one finds, in fact, that there is a much deeper faith, and indeed a certain relish in the largeness of the problems. And I began to feel, particularly after reading Mailer, that what looked like concern wasn't really concern but somehow seemed to come out of a type of boredom, a sense that life is going nowhere. To have a cause was a form of intellectual self-cherishing. Is this too cruel?

LOWELL: Well, I think something's wrong. I've just been to two countries very unlike the United States, Israel and Spain. One country I saw rather thoroughly—I met everybody I wanted to in Israel. In Spain I met nobody but just travelled at my pleasure with my family. You immediately feel that there are innumerable irritating things about Israel, but the problems you have here, of lack of faith and strife and chaos within the country, don't exist there. While it can be exaggerated, our Vietnam is an important, horrible thing. But we'd be in almost the same situation without it. And so it's quite mysterious what has caused this situation. I think what has caused it is the terrible danger of atomic destruction, and the failure on the whole to master our machinery, to use machinery to make life attractive, and to master birth control.

—What is your reaction to Mailer's description of yourself, to your first appearance as a fictional character in The Armies of the Night?

LOWELL: His description of me is one of the best things ever written about me, and most generous—what my poetry is like and that sort of thing. He records a little speech I made about draft-dodgers and I felt he was very good on that. I am trying to think whether my reaction to the march differed from his. I don't think mine was at all his, but it's not opposed to his either. It was mainly the fragility of a person caught in this situation . . . as in that poem of Horace's where you throw away your little sword at the battle of Philippi and get out of the thing. But I believe in heroic action too.

—I was wondering whether you felt a work of art could be achieved outside an accepted framework of values.

LOWELL: Do you think any primitive art is without a moral framework?

—No, I think it is guided by all sorts of taboos and it has all sorts of purposes.

LOWELL: Now say there's some bad, new sort of play where everyone undresses and copulates on the stage. Is that without moral values or is it just without art? I think it probably has moral values but doesn't have any art.

—I can imagine people undressing in a certain play which is linked or tied to something. But I asked this because I felt that perhaps satire—true satire—is impossible when values have been rejected.

LOWELL: Is it true that most, or all, satirists are conservatives?

—Absolutely, absolutely.

LOWELL: I think that the greatest ones of our time—Ring Lardner, parts of Genet probably, Wyndham Lewis, Waugh—are all conservatives.

—Instead of satire, one frequently has—if people are complaining or protesting—a dramatisation of the self. I find this quality, which I can only describe as egoism, coming through a lot in American writing, and I was wondering how far egoism reflects the American tradition. Most people seem to find life in America rather boring, they wish to step outside, they wish to express themselves, and the artist as egoist steps forward, like Mailer.

LOWELL: Do you think my writing has that sort of narrowness?

—When I say "egoism" I mean this: all its values somehow reflect a direct personal judgment on the way the world damages or the way the world pleasures the self. The other sort of writing is the writing that turns experience into something for all.

LOWELL: I remember reading something by Harold Rosenberg, a preface to a new translation of *The Idiot,* and he says this novel is very odd, that the hero is a spectator, you might almost say a voyeur. But he is conversed with and he's not a voyeur in the bad sense of the word, peeking on people. I'd like to appear as a voyeur in my poems, as someone watching rather than as someone running for Mayor of New York. That seems proper.

—Do you think it's a passing phase, this egoism?

LOWELL: Of my contemporaries in poetry or prose Mailer is the most talented. There's an awful lot of fat in his writings but there's an awful lot of courage, and the ambition, I think, is correct. You should try to be something. As long as he does immerse himself in things, and write three or four bad books, then write a true book. If he didn't write the true book, then the whole thing would just be pitiful and disgusting. But he does.

—You've made your life your work. You've written this long autobiographical novel, one might say, and the feeling that comes out at the end is one of pessimism, and yet this is accompanied by a very fine work of art, which, in fact, is a type of action. Are you aware, when you are actually doing the work, of a struggle between the pessimism and the effort that goes into creating the work itself?

LOWELL: You ask me about pessimism. I'm not sure what the word means, in the sense that I don't see why anyone would want to *intend* pessimism or optimism. You think of what you feel, then you're very astonished that what you feel falls into a groove that maybe you didn't intend. At the end of my last book I wrote this sentence, which is true but I don't understand why: "In truth I seem to have felt mostly the joys of living; in remembering, in recording, thanks to the gift of the Muse, is the pain." I really can't tell, reading my poems, whether they're outrageously optimistic or monotonously pessimistic. You try and do the best you can, and if it comes out sour you have to stay with that. You seem to falsify a poem by improving the mood.

—Tell us about Robert Frost.

LOWELL: He was actually the first important poet I met. He was lecturing at Harvard and I was, I think, a freshman. I was writing a tremendous poem in blank verse on the First Crusade, and I thought he'd like to see that. So I went round to see him and he was very nice. He read about half a line, then he got out the *Oxford Book of English Verse* and he showed me a poem by Collins, "How Sleep the brave by all their country's wishes blest." He said something like: "This is not very deep, but it's concise." Then he read me the opening of Keats's "Hyperion," which wasn't in the *Oxford Book,* I think, couldn't have been, and which I thought was all marvellous—a real tonic thing. He hit the line, "No stir of air was there . . ." and he said, "Now it comes to life," and he was right. "The naiad pressed the cold reed to her lips"—something like that. It was the best reading I had ever heard: about 12 lines he'd read, and he showed me two lines which made all the other lines come to life. I'd never encountered anyone like that. I saw him about every two or three years. He had no interest, not only in younger poets, but in any poet living besides Frost, and he was a terribly vain man. If you said something about *Moby Dick,* he'd mention Melville's short story "Bartleby" as his favourite—it was more the likes of what Frost did himself. I won't tell about when Pasternak got the Nobel Prize and Frost's reactions. On a small scale he had the sort of quality that Gorky describes in Tolstoy. He was beyond the good and evil of the druidic rock that stood there . . .T. S. Eliot was my hero in a way. I don't think he's the best poet of the century, but a very great one—on this point he's my hero. He had a very narrow gift, I think, but he wrote, until he was about 55, great poems, most of them quite long, an almost unexampled record in English. And he never quite wrote the same poem, partly by changing the metrical form, partly by changing himself, so it's the one man going from *Prufrock* through to the *Quartets.* Well, my thing is much less perfect than Eliot's. I have a lot of poems that are repeat poems. If you write a number of short poems, they're bound to be. There's a kind of model. I almost think I'm more varied than Eliot but much more repetitious. Yet I do think my books have changed. My first poems were very highly wrought: they were a young man's poems written during the war. Then, after a while, I wrote a very simple book called *Life Studies:* most of it is almost as simple as prose, in the sense that it could be read aloud and gotten on the first reading. It's about direct experience, and not symbols. It's terrible if you're bound to photograph your past, which I think I was doing in *Life Studies.* It's a decent book, but I don't want to write another *Life Studies.* Of course, you cheat and change things in giving what is supposedly the true story of your mother and father. But on the whole it seems as if it exactly happened in that kind of language.

John R. Reed

Going Back: The Ironic Progress of Lowell's Poetry

The general movement of Robert Lowell's poetry has been in ironic contra-diction to the conventional pattern of artistic development. The titles of three of his most important collections illustrate this tendency. From *Life Studies* to *Imitations* to *Notebook, 1967-68,* he has progressed from finished subject to raw material in a manner that would surely unsettle Sir Joshua Reynolds. Reynolds thought he was safe in recommending that all artists

From *Modern Poetry Studies,* I (1970), 162-81. Reprinted by permission of the journal.

accept a regimen that first provided them with a command of the "language" of their art and then allowed them "to amass a stock of ideas" which would be assembled according to the example of masters in their field. In a final stage, the aspiring artist could forego imitation, since he would now be emancipated "from subjection to any authority but what he shall himself judge to be supported by reason." He would no longer compare products of art with one another but examine "art itself by the standard of nature." The correct sequence of growth would seem to require that the artist begin with his sketches or notebooks, progress to imitations of acknowledged masters, and finally give his own peculiar style and talent free play in "life studies." But this can only be the case if the artist, like the typical student Reynolds was addressing in his discourse, conceives of experience as stationary, accessible, and potentially governable. When, however, as seems to be the case with Lowell, the subject matter of art is more elusive than its skills, when the "standard of nature" and the "stock of ideas" are more difficult to define than the method of definition, then some radical revision of the ordinary procedure is necessary.

Lowell's poetic growth does, in one way, follow Reynolds' prescription. His first published poems were in strict form that showed his command of the "language" of his art. He modelled himself on reputable fellow artists and achieved his own particular style, presenting art according to his own "standard of nature." The irony I mentioned earlier is in the fact that, as his mastery over his art increased, Lowell abandoned more and more of its identifying features until, like Michelangelo, he seems at times to be leaving us poems only half-emergent from the pages as the great sculptor left rough figures half-encaged in stone. This contradiction is not uncommon among artists. Although some move from a rough-hewn adolescent art to greater formal grace, others depart from classic form to test mature abandon. With Lowell, the attempt to define man's contest with experience determines the movement of his art.

In his great autobiography, Goethe recounts his youthful search for a definition of experience. Eliciting only mockery from his friends, he sought the answer from a military officer whom he had heard praised as a "sound-minded, and experienced man." From this gentleman's response the young Goethe concluded that "little better was to be gathered than that experience convinces us that our best thoughts, wishes, and designs are unattainable, and that he who fosters such vagaries, and advances them with eagerness, is especially held to be an experienced man." Pressed further by the enthusiastic poet, the officer gave the following concise definition: "experience is nothing else than that one experiences what one does not wish to experience." The young Lowell seems to have been less naive than the young Goethe, for his poetic career opened in *Land of Unlikeness* with a searing acknowledgment of the gulf between men's "best thoughts, wishes, and designs" and their attainment. And it is clear from a poem as early as "A Suicidal Nightmare" that Lowell's fundamental attitude toward experience was that it is essentially "what one does not wish to experience." This attitude must only have made the pursuit of what I have, for present purposes, termed "experience" more complex. More than one approach would have to be tried.

Jerome Mazzaro has described in *The Poetic Themes of Robert Lowell* the attempts Lowell made to surround experience—from the early epical approaches through the dramatic and narrative and finally to the imitative and personal. But despite the variety of his assaults upon experience, Lowell's struggle remained largely the same. In *Everything To Be Endured: An Essay on Robert Lowell and Modern Poetry,* R. K. Meiners contends that "the fundamental situation, the relationship of the self and the world, has remained essentially the same throughout Lowell's poetry." Jay Martin's brief study, *Robert Lowell,* more specifically asserts that Lowell's "basic subject has always been the fate of selfhood in time, and his basic method the examination of the convergence in man of past history and present circumstance." In *Robert Lowell: The First Twenty Years,* his early study of Lowell's poetry through *Life Studies,* Hugh Staples said that "Lowell's conclusion is that the human desire to preserve the sense of self-identity runs counter to the will of God"; and perhaps this explains why, in his subsequent poetry, Lowell has emphasized the view "that rapport with one's fellowman and not with God is the basis of man's new escape from time," as Mazzaro puts it in *The Poetic Themes.*

In any case, if Lowell's view of human experience is that it is "what one does not wish to experience," it is important to consider the nature of the self that must endure the experience. Staples saw that self in the early works as primarily a central theme of art, and, for him, Lowell's "career is the history of his gradual delimitation of his subject, which ultimately becomes himself." But for Meiners, "Lowell's poetry begins at the end of an era, where poetry has moved nearly as far into the person as it can go," and, by the time of *Near the Ocean,* that poetry has no challenge or vitality but "only nostalgia" because "the self has finally met circumstances too strong to be withstood." The tendency, then, among commentators is to see Lowell driven or advancing inward to a center of the self which is either negative and debilitating or consolidating and temperate. The implied metaphor offers us a picture of the poet gradually besieged by his own consciousness until he is cut off from his environment. My own feeling is that Lowell's career describes quite a different progression. As his views regarding the nature of human experience change, his poetry moves further from the obvious idioms of art and more toward the substance from which that art derives. He has, in a sense, "grown through art to life," as Martin suggests. He has ceased to be the formal artist who finished the portraits of *Life Studies* and has become the vehicle of experience himself in *Notebook, 1967-68.*

Very early in his poetic career, Lowell wrote "Most wretched men / Are cradled into poetry by wrong; / They learn in suffering what they teach in song," and thereby identified experience, education, and growth with suffering. Suffering was inevitable in a "land of unlikeness" where spiritual decay was almost universal and only the poet's "memory of the spiritual dignity of man," as Allen Tate put it in his preface to the collection, contended against it. But in cherishing the memory of man's spiritual dignity, the young poet was also assuming a more or less static moral world, a world in which designs played an important part and in which poetic form could temporarily replace a lost moral order. Consequently, in his early poetry Lowell sought to give his work cosmic dimensions through typology and symbolism. Man's decay was a result of his entrapment in the time-betrayed existence and, therefore, Lowell seems, as Mazzaro says, "to make 'escape from time,' regardless of its purpose, the aim of many of his heroes." In "From the Kingdom of Necessity," Randall Jarrell also suggests that a dominant impulse of the poems was toward liberation, but he identified confinement too much with social institutions. Numberless forces confine and oppress man, not least his own imaginings, and what Lowell, especially in *Lord Weary's Castle,* tries to break free from is less the institutions he deplores than that quality in himself that bears the spoiled seed of a sinful world. In the book's dedicatory epigraph, he prays "ita nos devotio reddat innocuos," which Staples renders, "so may our devotion free us of sin." But freedom from sin, in the sense that Lowell seems to mean here, involves a corresponding liberation from disgust. It means a careful acceptance of the meanness of this world. In the early poems, he struggled to make this acceptance indirectly through historical allusion and myth.

Lord Weary's Castle is a sequence of failing prayers, properly illuminated by the two poems drawn from Jonathan Edwards' writings. In "Mr. Edwards and the Spider," Lowell rearranges passages from Edwards' works to ask "What are we in the hands of the great God?" and then respond, "Your lacerations tell the losing game / You play against a sickness past your cure. / How will the hands be strong? How will the heart endure?" When the energy of the surprising conversion to faith passed, it may have been for Lowell as it was for Edwards' followers in "After the Surprising Conversions": "we were undone. / The breath of God had carried out a planned / And sensible withdrawal from this land." Without God, what does a God-designed world of pain and suffering portend beyond an invitation to die? The answer comes, after the false attempts to outmaneuver the problem by approaching it through the indirections and personae of *The Mills of the Kavanaughs,* in a collection whose title is richly suggestive, *Life Studies.*

In "Robert Lowell and the Poetry of Confession," M. L. Rosenthal has claimed that "Robert Lowell's poetry has been a long struggle to remove the mask, to make his speaker unequivocally himself." It could equally be claimed that Lowell's struggle has been to find a suitable mask for the rendering of a changing experience. In the poetry before *Life Studies,* he pictured man in a rigid world governed by the abused imperatives of God or the inescapable impulses of history. In *Life Studies,* he turned with dogged respect to face a world where man could only play a "losing game" because the "breath of God" had withdrawn. The works in this collection are not merely, as Rosenthal says, "a series of personal confidences, rather shameful" but a determined examination of a new world that has to be lived in. Commentators have been correct in reading the opening poem, "Beyond the Alps," as a farewell to a faith-governed view: "Much against my will / I left the City of God where it belongs." But it is worth remarking where Lowell goes when he turns his back on Rome. He goes into the "secular, puritan, and agnostical" night of "Skunk Hour," where he himself said that he sought to find "a way of breaking through the shell of [his] old manner," and of achieving a certain freedom in "the march and affirmation, an ambiguous one," of the skunks at the poem's end.

"Skunk Hour" is important not only because it is a good poem but also because it is a firm acceptance of the things of this world in all their ambiguous excellence. The figures of the past who open the poem are doomed and disappearing; the "fairy decorator" is caught in a meretricious existence between a fruitless profession and a presumably fruitless prospect of marriage. As Lowell succinctly states, "The season's ill." The speaker in "After the Surprising Conversions" described the man whose "thirst for loving shook him like a snake," though "he durst / Not entertain much hope of his estate / In heaven." The speaker in "Skunk Hour" shares that thirst for love and, hence, his quest on the golgotha of this earth for "Love, O careless Love." He provides an answer to the question: Why is this earth a place of pain? The speaker sees, "I myself am hell; / nobody's here—." No deity need have withdrawn; man's suffering is man-made, man-conceived, and what is most important, man-alterable. The skunk's "moonstruck eyes' red fire" makes the "chalk-dry and spar spire / of the Trinitarian Church" seem hollow and irrelevant. Nobody's here. The mother skunk and her family are neither intimidated nor frightened by the vacuity of this world; they have occupation enough in searching "for a bite to eat" in "the garbage pail." The mother skunk feasts freely "and will not scare." If man could find his sustenance as freely in a corrupt world, he, too, would not scare. The skunks, in an obscure way, have become hopeful models, and the speaker of the poem can stand on the "back steps and breathe the rich air." The commitment to and acceptance of the meanest level of existence is in itself a liberation from an ill season and a moral world that seems unoccupied.

The volume turns back then farther than Yeats's "the rag and bone shop of the heart" to the very blood and mire of material existence. His "mountain-climbing train" having "come to earth," Lowell can acknowledge in "Colonel Shaw and the Massachusetts' 54th," "I often sigh still / for the dark downward and vegetating kingdom / of the fish and reptile." The statue of Colonel Shaw stands as representative of man's human rather than spiritual dignity. As in *Land of Unlikeness,* the earthly kingdom has been transformed to mechanical servility by man and is threatened by moral collapse, but human not divine integrity constitutes the one tenuous force capable of resisting the moral decay. Colonel Shaw "is out of bounds now. He rejoices in man's lovely, / peculiar power to choose life and die." As Mazzaro suggests of *Life Studies,* it "is as if Lowell has discovered that he has begun too high on the scale of love and must take a step backward." In an interview with Frederick Seidel, published in *The Paris Review* in 1961, Lowell, explaining what he aimed for in poetry, began with his admiration for Tolstoi, whose "work is imagistic, it deals with all experience, and there seems to be no conflict of the form and content. So one thing is to get into poetry that kind of human richness in rather simple descriptive language." He said of the poetry of his own time, "It's become too much something specialized that can't handle much experience. It's become a craft, purely a craft, and there must be some breakthrough back into life." Lowell admired and shared Delmore Schwartz's desire for "openness to direct experience" and sought to break free into a medium more suited to that direct experience. "I couldn't get my experience into tight metrical forms," he explained.

What Lowell did not indicate in this interview was that his poetic form no longer could contain his experience because his experience, in certain ways, had changed. As I have already suggested, his early poetry is composed with the apparent assumption that poetic rule and law approximate moral rule and law. Mazzaro in "Robert Lowell's Early Politics of Apocalypse" has abundantly demonstrated the complex method by which Lowell, in his role of prophet, had "to distort the experiential, temporal, operative world about him into an immediately significative, atemporal, and thematic one." A formal metrical scheme is appropriate for his typological attempts to equate man-in-time with timeless truth. But, as experience proves less and less orderly, a surrogate mythology takes the place of moral archetypes, and, finally, beginning with *Life Studies,* but continuing in *For the Union Dead* and *Near the Ocean,* man's individual history is given meaning by associating it with all of human history. The brutal Old Pharoahs' monument only served to attract thieves, just as in New York "We beg delinquents for our life. / Behind each bush, perhaps a knife; / each landscaped crag, each flowering shrub / hides a policeman with a club." Violence and coercion are as eternal as anything man has to offer. No myths or symbols are necessary.

In dealing with the question of whether his poems are religious or not, Lowell said: "My last poems don't use religious imagery, they don't use symbolism. In many ways they seem to me more religious than the early ones, which are full of symbols and references to Christ and God. I'm sure the symbols and the Catholic framework didn't make the poems religious experiences. Yet I don't feel my experience changed very much. It seems to me it's clearer to me now than it was then, but it's very much the same sort of thing that went into the religious poems—the same sort of struggle, light and darkness, the flux of experience. The morality seems much the same. But the symbolism is gone." There may not have been much of a change, but it was enough to eliminate the old framework altogether and to put a new one in its place. The new method was an attempt to command personal history by finishing it. Stephen Spender observed in "Robert Lowell's Family Album" that the finality of Lowell's characterizations was both a strength of and a danger to the poetry of *Life Studies;* but, without an image of perfection elsewhere, it became necessary for Lowell to express the most rudimentary sense of completeness that he knew. This sense was in objects; in things that had been a part of his personal experience.

Major Mordecai Myers' portrait is the object that prompts Lowell's investigations of the things of his past in "91 Revere Street." The portrait "has been mislaid past finding," but it, in its Revere Street setting, is now "fixed in the mind, where it survives all the distortions of fantasy, all the blank befogging of forgetfulness. There, the vast number of remembered *things* remain rocklike. . . . The things and their owners come back urgent with life and meaning—because finished, they are endurable and perfect." In some poems—for example, "My Last Afternoon with Uncle Devereux Winslow"—objects are offered by themselves, in remembered groupings, to bear their own weight, simply evoking the sense of concrete existence. The "stogie-brown beams; fool's-gold nuggets; / octagonal red tiles," or the "Rocky Mountain chaise longue, / its legs, shellacked saplings," and the "almost life-size" posters, seem ultimately more permanent than Uncle Devereux, who is dying and will soon "blend to one color."

It would not have been inappropriate for Lowell to entitle his collection *Portraits,* since so many of the poems are mainly that; but his own title has a richer significance. Life studies in an art school generally represents the completion of apprenticeship and the initiation of personal contributions. In a sense, Lowell could be implying by his title that what preceded was apprentice work and only now was he turning to direct experience directly. At the same time, however, the sense of direct experience is conveyed, largely through departed persons and inanimate objects, and the final impression one receives is not of figures alive and moving but of specimens, trapped, finished, immobilized by art. The irony seems quite intentional. Staples feels that "Lowell's whole concern in these poems seems to be to arrest the flux of the actual, and, by so doing, to bring a measure of order and meaning into a transitional period of his career." Lowell's purpose was for Staples, "to defeat time, to give experience meaning through art, until remembered impressions because [sic] 'rocklike' and imperishable." Even before the volume Jarrell had noted Lowell's ability to convey "the contrary, persisting, and singular thinginess of every being in the world." And Martin, considering Lowell's more recent poetry, concludes that he has now become dependent upon objects: "What remains for the poet who has been made aware of the degradation of his democratic dogmas is his continuing ability to perceive (even to pity) the planet, to discover individual objects worth observing and naming, and to give them permanence through memory, and so preserve the self by its attachment to itself through things."

But Lowell himself appears to have been fully conscious of the relationship of things-in-themselves to things-in-poems. When Seidel asked him about the importance of detail in poetry, Lowell replied, "Some bit of scenery or something you've felt. Almost the whole problem of writing poetry is to bring it back to what you really feel, and that takes an awful lot of manoeuvering. You may feel the door-knob more strongly than some big personal event, and the door-knob will open into something that you can use as your own." And later, in describing how he came to write "Skunk Hour," Lowell said, "I was haunted by an image of a blue china doorknob. I never used the doorknob, or knew what it meant, yet somehow it started the current of images in my opening stanzas." Ultimately he did use the doorknob, though he had second thoughts about it, and, when "Waking Early Sunday Morning" appeared in *Near the Ocean,* the following stanza did not:

> Empty, irresolute, ashamed,
> when the sacred texts are named,
> I lie here on my bed apart,
> and when I look into my heart,
> I discover none of the great
> subjects: death, friendship, love and hate—
> only old china doorknobs, sad,
> slight, useless things to calm the mad.

Here is the "rag and bone shop of the heart" indeed. But Lowell does not presume that all begins there, for the objects cluttered in his heart also clutter all of existence. The universality that he sought in symbols, archetypes and historical allusions and parallels, is best represented, after all, by mere things in themselves. In *Life Studies*, Lowell sought to fix the past by designing portraits composed of the already perfected objects of the past. His poems aspired to the condition of Mordecai Myers' lost portrait. Then objects were anchors. By *Notebook, 1967-68*, Lowell is prepared to group all earthly things in the same "horrifying mortmain of ephemera," since all the remembered objects are no more significant than those who remember. "They go a-begging; without us, they are gone." Nonetheless, the poems are weighted with objects, sometimes listed out of sheer pleasure, it seems; Lowell can honestly state in a favorable summary of himself, "I never thought scorn of things."

This increasingly overt fascination for things in themselves is a sign of Lowell's compromise with existence. In the early works, objects served artistic purposes, often bearing symbolic burdens. Now they are part of the poem's texture of reality. To a great extent they mean only themselves. In the "finished" work of *Life Studies,* things and their owners, because finished, were "endurable and perfect." By *Notebook, 1967-68,* Lowell seems to have abandoned his early desire to escape time and acknowledges:

> Life by definition must breed on change,
> each season we scrap old cars and wars and women.
> But sometimes when I am ill or delicate,
> the pinched flame of my match turns living green,
> the cornstalk in green tails and seeded tassel . . .
> Only a nihilist desires the world
> to be as it is, or much more passable.

It is an uneasy, but resigned resolution between acceptance and ideal. The sentiment is repeated in a slightly irreverent echo of the classical dictum, "ars longa, vita brevis," where even the perfection of finished things seems to be abandoned in "this life too long for comfort and too brief / for perfection." Nonetheless, the affirmation that Lowell comes back to is still that of "Skunk Hour" and "Beyond the Alps." It is a grim and ambiguous affirmation, but it is there. "Everything points to non-existence except existence," he says in "Dies Irae, A Hope."

If Lowell was capable of demythologizing objects, he was also capable of extricating himself from the implications of family history. In *Life Studies* he began to draw himself away from the suffocating presence of his forebears. That may be another meaning in his title; from under the dead hand of history he felt himself emerging into life. "The nineteenth century, tired of children, is gone. / They're all gone into a world of light; the farm's my own." However, this reference by borrowing in Lowell's "Grandparents" to Henry Vaughan's poem glorifying death as a release from a dull world, indicates that the release from history is far more than an emergence into life. Vaughan wrote: "They are all gone into the world of light, / And I alone sit lingering here! / Their very memory is fair and bright, / And my sad thoughts doth clear." The very thought of mortality clears the mind, yet faces it with the mystery of death. Hope and dismay are intermixed.

The desire to escape from time in the early poems involved not only an escape from mundane existence but from the sense that time was primarily past time. "During Fever" alters the preoccupation with the past by demonstrating its connection with what is to be. The speaker is at the bedside of his daughter who is ill and "mumbles like her dim-bulb father, 'sorry.' " Their penitential relationship lets him recall his mother, events and objects associated with her, and her relationship with her father. By the end of the poem, the mother has moved from parenthood to marriage to a childhood whose relationships resemble the situation on which the poem opens. By positing the similarity, the speaker hints at the probable course of his daughter's life. When men can see themselves and their children re-enacting the lives of their parents, they have moved from fear to compassion. The past becomes another thing that is gone—a collection of portraits, like that of Mordecai Myers, to muse over but no longer to rage against. In *For the Union Dead,* Lowell is able to declare of "those before us": "we have stopped watching them." He has become aware of the real source of his dread, which is less in history— cosmic, earthly, or familial—than in self. In "Night Sweat," he admits, "But the downward glide / and bias of existing wrings us dry— / always inside of me is the child who died, / always inside of me is his will to die." The recognition of this resistless downward glide with its inevitable suggestion of repeated cycles of being leads him to pity those he most vehemently struggled against:

> At every corner,
> I meet my Father,
> my age, still alive.
> Father, forgive me
> my injuries,
> as I forgive
> those I have injured.

These self-conscious echoes of Christ's last words and the Lord's Prayer in "Middle Age" convey as well as anything else in the poem that we are indeed in the "secular, puritan, and agnostical" world of Lowell's maturity. As in "Skunk Hour," nobody's here; no God the Father, no Christ, only ourselves and our paradigms.

As a finished artist, then, who had abundantly demonstrated his ability with life studies, Lowell began to devote a considerable amount of creative energy to imitations of other poets' work. On the surface, this emphasis seems like an accomplished student's backward step to an earlier stage of learning; and, in an important way, that is what happens for Lowell. He has been composing imitations from the beginning of his career, and some of the reasons for his concentration upon rendering others' poems into his own English were academic, having to do with the university classes he was teaching. Nonetheless, Jarrell was unquestionably correct when he remarked that Lowell's period pieces and translations "both are valuable ways of getting a varied, extensive, and alien experience into his work." As Irvin Ehrenpreis puts it in "The Age of Lowell," "Lowell now set about discovering his own qualities in the whole range of European literature." Worth observing is that the poets to whom Lowell turns are for the most part men for whom experience meant "nothing else than that one experiences what one does not wish to experience." As Lowell admits in the Introduction to *Imitations,* the "dark and against the grain stand out." Since experience in his mature poetry must be viewed from a human perspective only, he seeks congenial outlooks. He no longer requires an Anne Kavanaugh, a Michael, or an old man drowsing over his Vergil. Now, when he wishes to convey another view of experience, he can do so openly, yet with his own voice. The experiences of others become his own expressions. His *Imitations,* he points out, "should be first read as a sequence, one voice running through many personalities, contrasts and repetitions."

Imitations in art serve the purpose of teaching not only technique but a way of perceiving. Roger Bowen in "Confession and Equilibrium: Robert Lowell's Poetic Development" states that "Lowell's progress is one toward two freedoms; one from the pressure of personal neuroses and an obsessive involvement with personal history, and the second from the diverting pressure of form." By *Life Studies,* Lowell seems to have been confident of technique; what he required was a wider experience, preferably not his own, to test the style that was ultimately designed to interpret direct experience. Martin explains: "After the completion of *Life Studies* Lowell felt emptied of self, uninterested in individuality. 'Something not to be said again was said,' he wrote to M. L. Rosenthal. 'I feel drained, and know nothing except that the next outpouring will have to be unimaginably different—an altered style, more impersonal matter, a new main artery of emphasis and inspiration.' " In "Reading Myself," Lowell has more recently confirmed this attitude. Speaking of his own writings, he says, "I memorized tricks to set the river on fire, / Somehow never wrote something to go back to." In *Life Studies,* Lowell made the "breakthrough back into life" that he felt was necessary for modern poetry. Having done so, he once more went to school to poets who themselves, in their own way, made their own breakthroughs into life. Lowell's next main step in this contradictory artistic movement was to return to the raw substance, the direct experience, the notes from which poetry draws its life.

In *Notebook, 1967-68,* Lowell takes his final step backward in his ironic progress and, in so doing, achieves one of his finest artistic productions. The old, finished style no longer works. "Sir Joshua Reynolds might retouch each fault," Lowell writes, implying at the same time that he has no such intention, largely because perhaps it is increasingly more difficult to distinguish faults from beauties. I do not mean to imply that the poems of *Notebook, 1967-68* are without art. In fact, once more the change, while not very great, is worth noting. The substantial number of references to portraits and depictions of one kind or another are sufficient to indicate a continued respect for formal modes of perception. But things have changed. The print of Waterloo that Lowell described in "Buttercups" appears again as "Waterloo," and the impression created by it is different. This "field of their encounter" now suggests "*La Gloire* changing to *sauve qui peut* and *merde.*" Familiar references to classical materials are still present, but they, too, have changed, as in the poem "Clytemnestra": "Orestes knew that Trojan chivalry was shit."

Lowell has always borrowed freely from sources. His detailed use of Jonathan Edwards' works have been indicated, and he acknowledges such borrowings as well as those in "Our Lady of Walsingham" and elsewhere. The borrowing continues, but another form has grown more and more common. In *Life Studies,* he made use of sources that can scarcely be considered in the province of belles lettres and which might be viewed as "found poetry." He describes, for example, the flyleaf in one of his father's books in "Father's Bedroom":

> "Robbie from Mother."
> Years later in the same hand:
> "This book has had hard usage
> on the Yangtze River, China.
> It was left under an open
> porthole in a storm."

Also, in that volume, in poems like "Ford Madox Ford" or "Commander Lowell," he began to use remembered conversations freely, and this has become, in *Notebook, 1967-68,* so common a technique that, although its use is clear in poems like "T. S. Eliot," "Ezra Pound," or "My Death," in some poems, especially ones like "Outlivers," private exchanges create certain difficult obscurities. Yet this willingness to use any fragments whatsoever that seem adequate for poetry is what makes the volume so much like an artist's sketchbook turned to masterpiece. It is, in some ways, like a painting by Larry Rivers, with public and private, completed and unfinished figures col-

lected together onto one canvas where they inconceivably produce a successful single work of art. In any case, Lowell has no foolish embarrassment
about the achievement. His explanation is matter-of-fact and slightly bored.
"I have taken from many books, used the throwaway conversational inspirations of my friends, and much more that I idly spoke to myself," he writes in
Afterthought. The poetic devices are the same, but the emphasis is more
toward the unfinished.

Lowell's poems since *Life Studies* have become generally more explicit, not
only concerning his private experiences, though notably with them. I am
convinced, however, that he is right to insist that a work such as *Notebook,
1967-68* "is not my diary, my confession, not a puritan's too literal porno-
graphic honesty, glad to share private embarrassment, and triumph." An indication of how, from one book to another, Lowell moves in the direction of
greater explicitness is the altered version of "1958" that appears in the collection. In *Near the Ocean,* the poem begins, "Remember standing with me in
the dark, / escaping? In the wild house?" The revised version simply says,
"Remember standing with me in the dark, / Ann Adden?" "Joan of Arc"
becomes "my Joan of Arc," and, after some other significant alterations,
Lowell ends the new version with the added line, "And if I forget you, Ann,
may my right hand...." Essentially the poem is unchanged regarding the
experience. Adding the identity of the person addressed is not confession so
much as canny poetic sense. A further indication of how eagerly and successfully he picks up any item of experience that moves him is his willingness to
adapt Ann Adden's reply as a companion poem "1968."

Nor should increased directness about sex be misconstrued as confession.
Lowell may write about "Going the limit on some slip of crabgrass ... or
once in New Orleans" in one segment of "Long Summer," but, as another
poem in the sequence declares, intensity of experience is matter for poetry in
any age: "The cattle get through living, but to live: / Kokoschka at eighty,
saying, 'If you last, / you'll see your reputation die three times, / and even
three cultures; young girls are always here.'" In "Redskin," Lowell describes
"love of the body, the only love man knows," and reminds us, in "Allah,"
that "woman wants man, man woman, as naturally / as the thirsty frog
desires the rain." He asks "who can help us from our nothing to the all, / we
aging downstream faster than a scepter can check?" No one is here to help
but ourselves; and we can help ourselves only if we recognize what we are.
Facing direct experience directly is the way. Lowell can exclaim, "all flesh is
grass, and like the flower in the field," then correct his biblical cliché, "no!
lips, breasts, eyes, hands, lips, hair." Moreover, though "aging downstream"
rapidly and dreading infirmity, he can acknowledge that infirmity is also "a
food the flesh must swallow, / feeding our minds ... the mind which is also
flesh." One of the great cries characterizing the collection occurs in the poem

"Hospital": "we need courses in life and death and what's alive." Lowell is ready to acknowledge and to use all experience. Even if "our best thoughts, wishes, and designs are unattainable" and experience is "what one does not wish to experience," it is possible still to entertain the designs and appreciate the experiences. Finally Lowell can say, "I am learning to live in history. / What is history? What you cannot touch." He is more than ever aware that "No moment comes back to hand, not twice, not once."

Earlier I quoted Jay Martin's statement that Lowell has "grown through art to life," but I do not mean to suggest that Lowell has, therefore, abandoned or lost faith in art. Poetry can break through to life without scrapping art. In fact, art may be precisely the means of making felt that experience men so eagerly crave. Art takes the raw experience and creates models; "the true Charles, done by Titian, never lived." In "The Vogue, the Vague," Lowell expresses concern about the point at which art falsifies life. "Was the captive chorus of *Fidelio* bound? / Does the painted soldier in the painting bleed?" he asks, trying to locate the reality of art. But, far earlier in the book he had answered that question. Sometimes the stereotype of thought or art is real, "life's lived as painted," though the one genuine model may leave nothing but "dynasties of faithless copies." The subtle relationship of these themes of art and life is supported by the construction of the volume as a whole, which gains meaning and form through a similar interrelation of motifs. Though the motifs that carry through the poem and illuminate the book as the "one poem" that Lowell wishes it to be considered are many, I shall give only one example and that briefly. Several colors recur in the volume, among them versions of red, green, gold, and black. Early in the book Lowell describes himself and a companion "greedily bending forward / for the first handgrasp of vermilion leaves." Reds often suggest intense experience of one kind or another, good or bad. But in the "dogdays and dustbowl" of this poem, men seem "like ears of corn, / fibrous growths . . . green, sweet, golden, black." Though all of these colors reappear significantly, I shall consider only the color green.

Youth and inexperience are, according to tradition, green. Lowell recalls when he "was lost and green" and characterizes a friend's youth as "sickly green." Greenness is, then, associated with youth, as in the first poem of the sequence "In the Forties." But it is also associated with death, with the "dead servant's green turf" or "the green grass" on which the wounded Roland faints. If all flesh is grass and the grass green, then men, like corn, may be reaped green or gold or black. So far, green proves evocative and ambiguous. It is more so when connected with vegetation—with real, waxen or disillusioned flowers—as it is consistently in the volume. I shall not trace these references here, since my main point is that green, the common symbol both of decay and growth, can beget corresponding sensations of disgust or hope. "The force that through the green fuse drives the flower / Drives my green age," Dylan Thomas wrote, and, using the color green in a motivic way himself in "Fern Hill," indicated that the child who was "green and carefree," "green and golden," was also "green and dying." Life is continual change but its ends may breed a kind of hope, "the pinched flame of my match turns living green, / the cornstalk in green tails and seeded tassel." Green may signify death, but, as over a field in Mexico "one sees the green dust as the end of life; / and through it, heaven," so in the ambiguousness of the color one may find hope.

There are further ambiguities in the color. The "green army" of peace marchers steps off hopefully, "like green Union Army recruits," to meet an opposing army wearing "green new steel" helmets. The marchers' inexperience and hope both prove too green, but surprisingly the decadent green of the new steel helmet suddenly proves hopeful, and Lowell exclaims, "health to the green steel head . . . to the kind hands / that helped me stagger to my feet, and flee." In "After the Convention," he writes, "life, hope, they conquer death, generally, always; / and if the steamroller goes over the flower, the flower dies. / Some are more solid earth." The young people in Chicago are neither inexperienced nor easily dismayed by disappointed hopes. This is no time for flowers; "under their bodies, the green grass turns to hay." If green represents life, hope, decay, and death because human existence is grass, corn, flower, and weed, how can man escape its terrible ambiguity? The answer is that he cannot. He can, in this life, simply accept, endure, and appreciate all that greenness means, all that life means. In another life, perhaps as seals, all could "take direction, head north—their haven / green ice in a greenland never grass." But that fancy is Yeats's dream of a Byzantium beyond terrestrial seas where he might be "a golden bird upon a golden bough." It is a nice, uncomplicated aim. Here nothing is so simple as that, nothing so easily resolved.

Lowell has moved from finished art that commands experience toward art that yields to the direct experience from which it arises. He has done so because he apparently no longer presumes to demand an order in existence, and is willing instead to accept whatever he finds in all its ambiguity and change. He began with experiments in free verse but, under the tutelage of figures like Tate, turned to strict forms in an attempt to control and command experience. Style alone does not provide such a command. His style has come, therefore, to flow with experience; his poetry to assume the idiom of event not of perception. His eager Catholicism may have been one mode of seeking salvation, but more than that, it seems to have been a means of commanding. By utilizing established religious symbols and archetypes, he sought to fit his experiences into a timeless pattern. Now it seems he has concluded that before man can achieve salvation, he must come to terms with the world of which he is a part. Before, the world was a theme that the armored spirit could discourse upon, but now the world is theme and matter, too. As Lowell said in "Skunk Hour," "I myself am hell; / nobody's here;" it's time to learn to "breathe the rich air" and "not scare."

Lowell began by assuming that his poetry could be inclusive of all his mental furniture and yet stand firm. Often the minds of characters and personae in his poems are fields of conflict in which a sentiment or emotion struggles to dominate rebellious experiences in retrospect. Especially in *The Mills of the Kavanaughs,* Lowell describes minds in the process of digesting what they have experienced. Along the way, however, too much of experience is lost or obscured by the mechanism that seeks to give it order. This mode of poetry would not have been suitable for Lowell for long, since it is difficult to imagine his own or any fictitious mind containing and governing the entire culture with which he is intimate. He attempted next to appropriate personal history by finishing it into acceptable portraits and to appropriate human history through allusion and the ventriloquism of translation. But finally, he seems to have concluded that one does not best represent individual experience by commanding it. Only through submergence in sensation or event does Lowell convey the direct experience in his poetry that he seems always to have wanted. Having got back past the paraphernalia of art to art's raw material, he appears to have abandoned the desire to dictate to experience and has, instead, accepted the humbler but more appropriate role of vehicle for experience. Now that we are back to the poet's notebook, we have no assurance that he will not turn again, but it is probable that henceforth we will have only notebooks to read from Robert Lowell.

Robert Boyers

On Robert Lowell

Decidedly, we do not live in "The Age of Lowell," despite what critics and others have recently said. Nor would it seem appropriate even to bestow the name of a lesser poet on so inglorious a period in man's history. Let us make no mistake about it: ours is the age of the Johnsons, the Nixons, a period in which what once seemed extraordinarily brutal or shoddy or banal now seems almost normal, certainly tolerable to most people. That is to say, we live at a time when it is remarkable that men of intelligence and compassion should bother to write poems at all; and that one or two should insist on creating great poems is a fact that imposes an unusual burden of gratitude on those of us who still care about such things.

It is difficult to know how anyone actually relates to a man like Robert Lowell. Certainly, for many of us, he is more than the sum of his poems, more a palpable presence than a tissue of convictions and doubts. We are aware of him always in his role as poet, but our notions of this role have distinctly expanded under the influence of his example. If Robert Lowell would not presume to accept Shelley's designation as "unacknowledged legislator of the world," he might lay claim to the office of unofficial spokesman to that small portion of the human brain we manage somehow to preserve against the clamor and violence that wither consciousness. Steadily, Robert Lowell has shown us not what it means to be a man in our time, for this we can know all too clearly by looking at ourselves, or at those around us; no, he has given us a portrait of a sensibility in retreat, in part from the world, but chiefly from the self he has become in response to that world. What we have come to expect from Robert Lowell in his poems and in his appearances before us as a man is a rather graphic demonstration of how little we have left that we can try to preserve. It may not be that what diminishes us as men is very much worse than what ordinarily diminished others in the past, but there is nonetheless a terror peculiar to our time. We know for certain now what diminishes us, and how, and perhaps even we know why, and still we cannot resist. How awful to know one's enemy, indeed to recognize him almost in every face one sees, to lack the grace and charity to turn one's cheek, and to want that faith and will which would permit one to strike back. There was a time, Lowell tells us in a poem, "when God the Logos still had wit/ to hide his bloody hands, and sit/ in silence, while his peace was sung./

From *Salmagundi,* No. 13 (Summer 1970), 36-44. Reprinted by permission of the author.

Then the universe was young." Now, as free as gods, though unable to decide how to use our freedom, and self-conscious to a fault, we fear our own potentially bloody hands, and mock the futility of our few commitments. Our prime gift, it would seem, is what Lowell has called "inexhaustible fatigue." Happy those growing multitudes of the sensitive and gifted whose negative capacities have not been thus limitless, and who have gratefully "dropped out" by whatever means they found available.

Those who have sought in Lowell's poems for strategies to ward off intimations of disaster, or metaphysical dread, have no doubt come away disappointed. When a fine poet-critic like Robert Bly complains about the failure of Lowell and his friends to achieve "a clear view of modern literature or politics," and about "their insistence on the value of alienation," he betrays expectations which measure the great distance between his own view of what is possible in the modern world, and Lowell's. In the view of Robert Bly and the gifted people around him, one decides either for or against alienation. One's poetry is either reducible to or suggestive of a program. One's emotional commitments are firm, rather than ambiguous, and doubts will disappear at the behest of will. Really, it is a most attractive way of looking at things, only of course it is but one way among many, and it is in the nature of human experience that those who believe such propositions as Bly's viable, will have an inordinate capacity for self-deception, or dishonesty. These are qualities conspicuously lacking in Robert Lowell, as even his severest critics have had to agree. And their absence has not made him or his work more appealing. Candor can become offensive when manifested at the expense of one's cherished illusions, and we are learning that it is possible to engage on behalf of human values while certain that on that field where battles are fought, values are as nothing, and engagement a hopeless gesture.

What is it then that has so drawn a generation of literate people to Robert Lowell? Certainly he has not courted favor as a hero, and the odd combination of hesitation, commitment, regret, disgust, reminiscence, and weariness one finds in his poems and public utterances does not give promise of heroic stature. Or does it? It may be that we have lately conceived another kind of hero than we once worshipped or imagined, not exactly an anti-hero, nor a proletarian everyman, but a victim, one who has not learned to cope to the degree that he has refused to compromise the clarity of his perceptions. His tragedy, if you will, is not that seeing clearly, he must lose his eyes, or wander friendless, but that he continues to see, to grow bored, and to be unable to turn away. Robert Lowell has been "our poet" because he has had trouble getting through each day, and told us why. We do not identify with him, we envy him foolishly, sentimentally, but definitively. He sees, and suffers, and we would suffer with him if only we could convince ourselves there were something in it for us. Ultimately, we decide, it is enough that Robert Lowell sees and suffers for us all, a distinction we might have permitted him to share with Sylvia Plath had she lived to a riper age.

It is an extraordinary relationship for a poet to have developed with his audience, and to maintain this relationship, Lowell has had to violate the integrity and unity of his personality. For some people, whether great or ordinary, a posture is a strategy which is followed or abandoned according to the exigencies of a given situation. In the case of Robert Lowell, the man has become the posture, and nothing in the poems or utterances rings false—but it is a posture that addresses us, a role, not a man. So perfect has been the assumption of this role that we rarely notice how it dictates gestures and commitments wholly at odds with the man's temperamental indisposition to indulge such things. What most of us applaud when he publicly insults the President of the United States, or counsels young men to resist the laws of their country, or storms the Pentagon, is his temerity and conscience. What we are less likely to consider are the doubts, the irony that are so much a part of the commitment, and which in fact call into question the very meaning of the various enterprises. But then, nothing has become more paradigmatically demonstrative of purity of intention in our time than failure, and those of us who have found even the lesser failures a bit more costly than we are willing to allow ourselves must often have silently thanked Robert Lowell for permitting us to deplore and pity his. He is our truest victim, for we have together cast him in such a way that he can only assuage, never goad. And if he has been a witting and willing accomplice in the entire operation, by so much has it been the worse for him. To be aware of the mechanism by which one is appropriated by an audience, is to understand how little that audience can deserve.

As it is, Lowell's generosity towards his audience, and towards those one could not ordinarily expect to distinguish between his poetry and any other body of work, is nothing less than a wonder. For it is not the kind of generosity that consorts with mere flattery or muddle-headedness. What it reflects, instead, is a terrible and unceasing sense of the poet's own complicity in the brutalities and casual cruelties to which his poetry bears constant witness. His latest volume, *Notebook 1967-68,** is in this regard a continuation of earlier volumes even as it introduces a whole number of considerations we have not encountered before in Lowell's work. He has, after all, always been concerned with varieties of victimization, as he is still, but such concerns are no longer mounted with such obsessional ferocity as they once were. The rage, the disgust, the self-loathing are still present, but a note of philosophic detachment has crept in. The grotesque particulars continue to abound, including apocalyptic blue-black flies, the corpse of Che Guevara "laid out on a

*Notebook 1967-68 by Robert Lowell, Farrar, Straus & Giroux, 1969 .

sink in a shed, displayed by flashlight-", and the embitteredly neurotic harangues of the aging William Carlos Williams. But these particulars work in the service of a vision that has somehow relaxed as its perspective has broadened. Lowell was always a rather learned poet, but the range of his language and the variety of his references in this new volume are an extension of what has come before, and where personal experience had always been evoked against the background of particular failed cultural institutions and inherited family hang-ups, Lowell here paints upon a canvas of limitless dimension. I am speaking, then, of a momentous shift in Lowell's entire conception of necessity, the consequences of which we can only begin to perceive in the present volume, but which clearly do not involve a reduction of those human sympathies Lowell has managed to retain despite great personal pain and loss. This shift is perhaps best examined in connection with a passage from one of Randall Jarrell's essays on another poet, W. H. Auden:

"He [Auden] is fond of the statement *Freedom is the recognition of necessity,* but he has never recognized what it means in his own case: that if he understands certain of his own attitudes as *causally* instead of logically necessary—insofar as they are attitudes produced by and special to his own training and culture—he can free himself from them. But this Auden, like most people, is particularly unwilling to understand. He is willing to devote all his energies and talents to finding the most novel, ingenious, or absurd rationalizations of the cluster of irrational attitudes he has inherited from a former self; the cluster, the self, he does not question, but instead projects upon the universe as part of the essential structure of that universe . . . it turns out that the universe is his own shadow on the wall beside his bed."

Now there are all sorts of assumptions implicit in Jarrell's remarks that we really have not the time to dwell upon in their generality. What seems clear is that Jarrell was largely right about Auden as a particular instance of a projection that in Auden's case was illegitimate because insufficiently understood as what it was, by the poet himself as well as by the majority of his readers. What is questionable at the very least is Jarrell's notion that to see attitudes as *causally* rather than as logically necessary is to have a lively possibility of freeing oneself from them. That it were true, is all one can say by way of general response. Who better than Lowell has seen the specifically *causal* necessity of his debilities, and how many among our poets of major stature in this century have had a more impossible time freeing themselves from the attitudes and anxieties causing them? Lowell has of course avoided the projection Jarrell attributes to Auden, a projection that has allowed for "rationalizations of the cluster of irrational attitudes," and the subsequent quietude that has made Auden seem so removed from many of us. Where Lowell has even suggested a necessary relation between the failures of culture and the despair of the self, he has done so with a vital sense of ambiguity, an awareness of perpetual tension between that self as source of the world's miseries and the self as victim of forces beyond its control. The freedom that Lowell's verse has always managed to nourish as a possibility is the freedom to see everything in its unrelieved complexity. The tightness and organization of his idiom has testified to the urgent complication of materials the contemporary artist must deal with, rather than to any desire to get away from the complexities of life.

The *Notebook* represents a shift which would seem to promise just that freedom Jarrell conscientiously refused to acknowledge as possible under such circumstances. For as Lowell's perspective has opened out, as he has learned to dwell upon a woe that is in no way time-bound or culture-bound but truly universal and for all time, his heart has lifted, his energies throb toward life as we cannot remember them doing in any previous volume going all the way back to *Land Of Unlikeness* in 1944. At the center of *Notebook* is still the self, its manifestation the peculiar speaking voice whose inflexions reverberate in the mind, all unmistakably resonant with echoes remembered from dozens of earlier poems. It is even in some sense an autobiographical volume, its pages filled out with many poems on Lowell's marriage, his daughter Harriet, even on the father whose memory Lowell clings to guiltily like the shadow of a debt never to be paid. But what is most impressive here is the poet's desire to deal with the history of his time, in this case the history of a single year, on its own terms. This is not a portrait of a sensibility in retreat, either from the world or the anguish of the stricken self. He can say in honesty and with relative confidence, knowing what he is about, "Still, it's a privilege to enter the bullring." For the first time in reviewing Lowell's volumes the reader has a sense of the poet as somehow equal to everything he describes, no matter how grisly. Though none of us including the poet is ever very far removed from the prospect of pain, he will have us understand that we ought to survive it, that we will. There is nothing especially brave in this—the tone is more quietly resolute and humbly human than we could have expected from the author of *Lord Weary's Castle,* and though one of his recent critics calls him a "magnificent curser," the presence that speaks through the pages of *Notebook* is better approximated by such lines as: " 'Better to die, than hate or fear,/ better die twice than make ourselves feared or hated' ". Gone for Lowell are the days "when hurting others was as necessary as breathing,/ hurting myself more necessary than breathing."

In charting a path away from the morbidly obsessional preoccupations with his own psyche, Lowell has had to project a vision of necessity much closer to what Jarrell claims was the undoing of Auden. But Lowell refuses ever to indulge anything like evasion rationalization, as we have suggested, and to the extent that Auden has found it possible to justify withdrawal from the arena of politics and history, Lowell has found it more and more possible to participate both actually and emotionally, though his awareness of attendant ironies and miscastings has in no way diminished. To the extent, that is, that Lowell has been able to see himself as a man among other men, subject to the temptations and disorders of an Agamemnon, a Napoleon, a Kennedy, a Robert Frost, rather than as a being peculiarly unsuited to vital existence by virtue of specific disorders associated with his own very special inheritance, he has been able to acknowledge and be grateful for those goodly dispensations that have come his way.

The freedom to dwell upon his own strength and relative happiness then, is a function of Lowell's hard-won recognition of necessity as the sign under which all men live, not some men, and there is in *Notebook* a very special awareness of the dangers implicit in the enjoyment of good fortune, in the cultivation of one's own health and resilience. The necessity that often encourages us to deal cruelly with one another need be no mere outgrowth of neurotic debility, but a certain unstable dynamic that enforces our radical isolation from others even as we reach out to touch them. One does not, under the force of such an impression, thereby cease to reach out, but one does so with a measure of hopeful resignation that might have amused Lowell twenty years ago. The almost gratifying tension is clear in lines from one of Lowell's poems on the Charles River: "The Charles itself, half ink, half liquid coaldust,/ testified to the health of industry—/ wrong times, an evil dispensation; yet who/ can hope to enter heaven with clean hands?" The particulars are all in place. Lowell is writing about his own time not as though it were simply reducible to those abstract universals by means of which men escape all sense of necessity as the density of circumstance crowding the subjective consciousness, pressing it for dominance in a constant dialectical interplay. But the detachment from sheer necessity, the sense of the self's contingent potency is nonetheless proven in the generalization ". . . who/can hope to enter heaven with clean hands?", which if it is not a logical culmination of preceding particulars is hardly in the nature of an afterthought, or a mere wishful projection of private need onto the structure of the universe.

The 274 "fourteen line unrhymed blank verse sections" that constitute *Notebook* are tremendously varied, but a number of impressions would seem valid for the sequence as a whole. For one thing, the structure of the sequence itself cannot but generate tensions of a peculiar sort, for while Lowell tells us that "the poems in this book are written as one poem," a number of them are so complete, so self-contained that one is loath to admit them into the jagged contours of the whole, to see them thus swallowed and perhaps obscured. The impression of the *Notebook* as a unity is bothered by pervasive discontinuities not so much in tone or language as in the levels of reality evoked, and these discontinuities are as present within the confines of single poems as they are in the sequence. One thinks for example of the piece called

"Che Guevara" which swings from the gaudy reality of Che's mutilated corpse laid out on display, to a casual love-tryst in, perhaps, New York's Central Park overshadowed by towering and unfeeling skyscrapers boding ill to human relationship, and finally to some ancient image of exiled kings hiding out in trees. It is all very colorful, and not a little pregnant with apparent significance, only the reality of Che is lost completely, and the feelings mentioned seem so impermanent, so arbitrary in the poem's structure that one cannot know what to make of them. We know very well what Lowell means when, in addressing his fellow poet in "For John Berryman," he writes: "John, we used the language as if we made it./ Luck threw up the coin, and the plot swallowed,/ monster yawning for its mess of pottage." Surely the marvelous richness of texture and virtuosity of metaphor in *Notebook* is a reflection of this compulsive originality in Lowell, his desire to preserve the mystery inherent even in the surfaces of events and things by avoiding the easy presentations we associate with prose accounts. But we may be permitted to wonder whether sheer chance ought legitimately to govern not only the concerns of a poem, but their concrete poetic manifestations as well. If in reading Lowell's "Che" we suspect the poet might have little difficulty in justifying the progression of details were he set upon to do so, we have certainly no reason to believe that he could not do as well justifying wholly disparate particulars.

Most of the poems in *Notebook* are, however, considerably more coherent, and many rank with the very best things Lowell has written. Underlying everything is this relatively new, unanticipated concern with health, strength, animal vitality, and their reflection on a political level in the perpetual exercise of power. We see it operating at once in the volume's opening sequence of four poems entitled "Harriet," concluding with the lovely and troubling reflections on what a parent ought to wish for his only child.

> The child of ten, three quarters animal,
> three years from Juliet, half Juliet,
> already ripens for the night on stage—
> beautiful petals, what shall I hope for,
> knowing one choice not two is all you're given,
> health beyond the measure, dangerous
> to yourself, more dangerous to others?

And we confront such notions again in the deeply moving poem on "Robert Frost," which concludes on the following exchange: "And I, 'Sometimes I'm so happy I can't stand myself.'/And he, 'When I am too full of joy, I think/ how little good my health did anyone near me.' " The political consequences of power are too often dwelled upon in our culture to require that we rehearse them in their abstract potentiality still again—as Lowell himself acknowledges in an earlier poem from *For The Union Dead,* we frequently open our eyes to realize that "we have talked our extinction to death," there referring to fears of nuclear calamity.

But what is new in *Notebook,* beyond the concern with power and health, the relation between personal vigor and political commitment, is the relative delight Lowell is able to take in things, in people, in the procession that is history, replete as it is with murder and disaster. He no longer seems to want to turn away from the gaudy spectacle, and the boredom that is consequent upon the turning in of all experience upon the relatively static responsiveness of the self has largely disappeared. There will never be anything remotely playful in Lowell's work, we may suppose, nor could we ever desire such a thing. But the degree to which he has here given himself to the contemplation and vivid evocation of realities beyond the twistings of his old self surely speaks optimistically of Lowell's own health and satisfaction with the fact and manner of his survival. If anything, his poetry has become a more comprehensive and essential document of civilized consciousness in the twentieth century, and its registration of fluctuations in conviction and hope is surely testimony to the relentless honesty of Lowell's work. If he can say at one point "it's the same for me/at fifty as at thirteen, my childish thirst/for the grownups in their open car and girls . . ." we know that he has won to better conclusions. What the critic F. W. Dupee wrote of Lowell's *Life Studies* upon its appearance ten years ago may perhaps be said of *Notebook,* but one would not, somehow, have Lowell any other way. "But given their [the poems'] intense response to what they describe, they suffer a little from being inconclusive as to the meaning of it all. Where, Henry James would inquire, is your dénouement?" Well, Robert Lowell is not Henry James, and perhaps it is not amiss to suggest that in the vision of life's possibility we share with Robert Lowell, and to which he is our most intelligent and consistent witness, we can not find anything like the dénouement James would have required. Surely it is not anything about which we can now afford to worry. There is a sense in which motion, process, the will to keep going, is all we have, very likely all we shall for some time need to have.